S0-BEF-888

Growing Up Twice:

Shaping a Future by Reliving My Past

By Aaron Kirk Douglas

Newsworthy
Books

Growing Up Twice: Shaping a Future by Reliving My Past

© 2015 Newsworthy Books
First edition published in 2016

All rights reserved. No part of this book may be reproduced or transmitted in any form or by any means, electronic or mechanical, including photocopying, recording, or by any information or retrieval system, without permission in writing from the publisher.

I have tried to recreate events, locales and conversations from my memories of them. In order to maintain their privacy in some instances I have changed the names of individuals and places, I may have changed some identifying characteristics and details such as physical properties, occupations and places of residence.

All reasonable, good-faith efforts were made to secure copyright permissions for images and text reproduced in this book.

Library of Congress Cataloguing-in-Publication Data

Douglas, Aaron Kirk, 1961-

Growing Up Twice: Shaping a Future by Reliving My Past

ISBN: 978-0-9970501-0-3

Cover design by Nehara Rathnamali
Development Editors: Jordan Crawford, Arthur Manzi
Edited by: Frank M. Young, Michael Munkvold
Photos © Aaron Kirk Douglas except as noted herein
Graphic design by Rob Ottley, Ottley Design Group

Newsworthy Books
editor@newsworthybooks.com
www.newsworthybooks.com

Printed in the United States

Contents

Author's Note

In America today, there are 4.5 million young people in a structured relationship program. An additional 16 million youth—including nine million at-risk youth—will reach age 19 without a mentor.·

As a mentor, I often look for resources to help me understand and respond to events and milestones in our relationship. While there are plenty of books advising how to mentor someone in the workplace, I haven't found a single memoir by a mentor of an at-risk youth. I thought perhaps there were people out there like me, who wanted to know what mentoring might *feel like*. And I wanted to see if there were resources I could learn from, in order to be a better mentor. The surprise, I think, is that if you're like me, mentoring doesn't just change a child's life—it can heal your own.

·Source: "The Mentoring Effect: Young People's Perspectives on the Outcomes and Availability of Mentoring." A report for MENTOR: The National Mentoring Partnership, (Jan. 2014) by Civic Enterprises in association with Hart Research Associates. Mary Bruce and John Bridgeland.

READER COMMENTS

This story made me want to call everyone I love and somehow make them understand what this book made me understand: that our relationships of love transcend everything else.

—Jennifer Brandlon, former AP Newswoman and Correspondent, The Oregonian

Growing Up Twice is surprisingly funny, melancholy and hopeful. Aaron Douglas has a novelist's eye for small but telling details, and his insight into the messy task of being a human being is impressive. More than a memoir, it's a guided tour of two Americas barely covered by the so-called mainstream.

—Frank M. Young, Award-winning author, artist and musician

Written in a contemporary American voice that's clear, easy to read, and engaging.

—Arthur Manzi, Writer/Editor

Dedication

Rico, 2006

Before meeting Rico, I hadn't been the type of person who cried a lot. My work with him changed that. It was a journey that became more joyful—and more painful—than anything I had ever experienced.

This book is dedicated to mentors of all stripes—to Bigs and Littles past and present—and to Rico, who after reading this, now knows how much he helped me too.

"Only a life lived for others is worth living."
—Albert Einstein

Introduction

One of my most important life lessons occurred early one June morning in 1992. Some friends and I were meeting in a small coffee shop nestled in the courtyard of the 5th Street Market in Eugene, Oregon. It was unusually humid, but the courtyard fountain's gurgles somehow made it feel cooler. We greeted each other, placed our drink orders, and sat in the shade at a black wrought-iron table.

When the barista called my name, I jumped to retrieve my coffee, and grabbed the thick white mug filled nearly overflowing with a quad-shot Americano. I sat the mug on our table.

I was tired and aching for coffee. I had been up all night on a bus from Seattle to Eugene. The bus had stopped in almost every town along the 300-mile route. The trip was made even more exhausting by a middle-aged blowhard in the front of the bus who talked to the driver incessantly. His voice bounced straight back to me in to the rear of the bus. It was impossible to sleep. My friends must have thought I looked like hell.

I was in town to visit my parents, whom I hadn't seen in many months. There was just enough time to meet my friends for coffee before heading across town to Springfield, where my parents were still living in the same house from my childhood.

Patricia and her husband patiently waited for me. It was a bad habit of mine to arrive five minutes late to everything, and today was no exception. I eagerly anticipated the first swig of that much-needed shot of caffeine. As the mug tipped to my lips, everything went black.

My friends later told me I fell back in my chair and turned blue, foamed at the mouth and flopped around on the ground.

My grand mal seizure scared the hell out of them.

What did I feel? Nothing. When I came to, and opened my eyes, there seemed to be a shift in the space-time continuum. I lay on a stretcher, and a paramedic stared back at me. He walked alongside me on the way to the ambulance.

"Do you know where you are?" he asked.

I knew where I was. Wait... where the hell was I, and why was I on a stretcher?

"Have you ever had a seizure before?" he asked.

"A what? —Uhhh, no." I replied, slowly figuring out why he was asking.

The paramedics dropped me off at the emergency room. I can't remember much of that morning. I know my parents showed up at the hospital, and that I cried. It was such a shock. I couldn't figure out why this had happened, or why chunks of time were missing from my memory.

Back in Seattle, a neurologist put me on Depakote, a drug with side effects that included weight gain, hair loss, suicidal thoughts, and the possibility of sudden death.

After that first seizure, three more followed. They all happened two years later, after I had tapered off the medication. I stopped taking the drugs because with epilepsy, it's sometimes possible for your brain to "unlearn" having seizures after a while.

I had the first of a trifecta of seizures as I was heading back with a friend to Seattle from a vacation in Ashland, Oregon. We drove for hours and finally stopped at a Starbucks an hour south of Seattle. Once again, just as I was about to drink my coffee, I had a grand mal seizure. As customers fled from the busy serving area, my friend yelled out to the baristas, "Dang, your coffee sure is strong!"

We went to the hospital in nearby Olympia, and I was told to go home and to see my regular doctor the next day.

Late that afternoon, another seizure struck. I hit my head on my bedroom doorknob. An hour later, I was in a Seattle ER. It was there that I had the worst seizure of all.

When we got to the ER, the doctor decided to set up an IV drip of Dilantin, an anticonvulsant medication. A while later he said we could go. As he gave us instructions for follow-up care, my eyes rolled up and I fell straight back. My skull slammed hard onto the cement floor. ("It sounded like a watermelon," my friend said later.)

As I woke up, the doctor leaned over me, and held me down by the shoulders, commanding me not to move. He thought I might have a concussion. I couldn't think straight. My fight-or-flight response kicked in. All I wanted to do was sit up. I tried to rise with every ounce of my strength, straining so hard that I was sweating through my clothes.

"We need you to stay down!" a nurse said. "You hit your head!"

The doctor leaned down close to me. "What year is it?"

Numbers floated around inside my head: 1974, 1972, 1977, 1979, 1981. Finally I guessed, "1983?" It was 1995.

The nurse and the doctor looked at each other. He spoke again: "Who's President of the United States?"

Dang. I voted. I should remember. Nixon? No. Carter? Wilson? Shit. They were all jumbled.

"Ronald Reagan!" I replied, trying to appear certain.

It was Bill Clinton.

It turned out that my skull was fine. I went home that night back on Depakote—the pills with all the side effects. They helped with the seizures, but did nothing to prevent the months of panic attacks that followed.

My biggest fear was that the pills wouldn't work—that I would fall down crossing the street and get hit by a bus. Or, worse yet, that I might accidentally kill someone with my car.

I didn't drive for a year.

It's been more than 20 years since that first seizure. Every morning, as two anticonvulsant pills sit on the counter, I have to stop for a moment and think.

I am faced with one of life's most unavoidable truths. None of us alive have any idea how much time we have left. None of us know when everything will go black. None of us have a choice.

Chapter 1

The Beginning:
Summer 2005

Life was full. My hectic schedule revolved around work, family, hobbies and some volunteer projects. After six years volunteering for the Epilepsy Foundation, and at Portland's historic Hollywood Theatre, I wanted something more.

One summer afternoon, at a riverfront festival in downtown Portland, I happened across a booth for the Portland chapter of Big Brothers/Big Sisters of America. A pleasant volunteer stood there, sweating in the hot sun. Seeing the booth reminded me of an editorial from a recent issue of the *Business Journal*. The publisher, Craig Wessell, had written extensively about how important Big Brothers/Big Sisters was to the community. It struck me as one of the most passionate things he'd ever written.

I turned around and went back to the booth.

"What's a Big Brother, exactly?" I asked.

"It's our term for a mentor—a person like a teacher, or a trusted friend," said the volunteer.

"What do you have to do?"

"Most of the children in our program have a lot of disruption in their lives," he said. "We look for volunteers who can spend a couple hours a week on activities or working on homework. The kids who come into our program need an adult who can help provide a sense of stability." He handed me a pamphlet. "They need someone to talk to."

Back home, I tossed the pamphlet on a side table. For the next several days, I thought about what it might be like to become a Big Brother. Despite having little opportunity to interact with children, I could get along with a kid. What could be so hard about that? Like many people, my life had a lot of upheaval. Still, I wondered if I were a good enough role model for a lonely child.

The pamphlet sat, undisturbed, on the counter for months. One day, I felt a sudden inspiration to complete my online volunteer application. It was quite detailed, and asked me about my employment history, academic achievements, hobbies and references.

My listed hobbies were filmmaking, photography, music, writing, swimming, hiking, and lifting weights. Perhaps they would match me up with a Little Brother (they called them "Littles") who liked those same things. I then laughed at the absurd idea of handcrafting a perfect child. That didn't seem likely.

About two months later, they said I'd passed the background check. It was time to attend an interview. A match specialist met with me for an hour, and talked with me—mostly about my motivation for wanting to be a Big Brother.

When the interview was over, the specialist told me it would take a few more months to find the right Little Brother for me. In the meantime, there was a required three-hour orientation. The meeting was quite detailed and included a training manual. The manual defined a Big Brother as "an adult friend, confidante, teacher, guide, supporter, and cheerleader." My stated objectives were to:

- Be consistent and reliable
- Be firm and set limits
- Avoid an emphasis on money
- Allow the relationship to develop gradually
- Maintain a "one-to-one" relationship
- Respect my Little Brother, and
- Be a friend and role model

In addition to these objectives, the 55-page manual included a list of do's and don'ts, along with definitions of the *Role of the Parent* and the *Role of the Match Specialist*. The match life cycle was said to include these stages:

- Early development
- Growth
- Maturity
- Leaving your Little, [withdrawal, avoidant behavior]
- Match closure could occur at the following times:
  o If one of us withdrew; or
  o If the match was closed for a rule violation; or
  o When the Little graduated from high school or turned 18 (whichever was later)

Our orientation included cultural awareness skills. We were expected to understand that our Little might not give us much credibility in terms of being able to relate to their particular culture. This was especially true around issues like communication styles, time orientation, lifestyle and social norms.

Having grown up in the Caucasian blue-collar town of Springfield, Oregon in the 1970s, it didn't surprise me that I might need education on cultural differences. Conversely, it seemed like I might need to educate my Little Brother on what it was like growing up in a bastion of conservatism, with a father who surrounded our entire family with his fondness for loud country music.

The training manual's positive communication skills included active listening, paraphrasing, door opening, asking questions, body language and talking about your feelings.

This relatively short list of positive communication skills was dwarfed by a catalog of negative communications. These included making accusations, irrational statements, rationalizing, giving orders, threatening, moralizing, lecturing, providing solutions, criticizing, psychoanalyzing, use of the silent treatment, cross-examining, praising ("When misused, praise implies the speaker is in a position to judge"), giving excuses and sympathizing ("these types of messages don't always express understanding and empathy").

Dang. This was going to be complicated. No psychoanalyzing? No praising? No lecturing?

Safety issues for Bigs and Littles covered motor vehicles ("safety belts are always required"), use of alcohol ("no drinking within four hours before or during an outing") and a strict warning:

"Any illegal activity such as letting the child drive without a permit/license is cause for immediate match closure."

We were told to identify signs of mistreatment, including inattention to basic needs and physical, emotional, or sexual abuse. Bigs were required by state law to report any sexual abuse to state Child Protective Services.

Other sections in the training manual covered discussions of sex education, when and where to change clothes, privacy for sleeping arrangements, appropriate physical touch (including body contact and wrestling) and the importance of avoiding relationship exclusiveness and over-involvement. Overnight visits were not allowed until after the one-year anniversary of a successful match.

The training manual advised Bigs to never keep secrets from parents or the match specialists. Likewise, Littles were told not to ask their Big to keep secrets. "All activities, conversations, etc. have to be considered open territory to a child's parent/guardian and case manager should the need arise."

These 55 pages of guidelines and restrictions made perfect sense, but contained a lot to absorb. I decided to purposefully pause for a moment to contemplate whether such a complex undertaking was right for me.

Moments such as these had a regular place in my day. I was raised a Southern Baptist, but had spent the last 22 years centering myself. I explored everything mystical I could get my hands on and had long been fascinated by numerology, astrology, mysticism, spirituality, the Kabbalah, and any mystics of the East. My search included two trips to India to see a living guru. Most recently I converted to Judaism, and had met people of that religion who fought for social justice.

Many years of meditation helped me develop a firm belief in karma—the idea that we deserve or want whatever happens in our lives in order that we might learn deep, meaningful truths. If ever there were an opportunity to test this belief, it was by becoming a Big Brother. Then, six months later, I met my match.

Chapter 2

The Introduction: June 2006

The Big Brother/Big Sister vetting process is never rushed. The specialists responsible for finding the right mentors for each child discussed "the art of the match" at my orientation.

Six months after my application, a date was set for formal orientation. They told me my Little's name was Rico. I learned he lived 25 miles away—a 90-minute round trip by car. For me a long drive to see any Little was inevitable. I lived on a houseboat on Sauvie Island—a huge pastoral land mass the size of Manhattan, located 12 miles west of downtown Portland.

The houseboat was moored on the Multnomah Channel—an offshoot of the Willamette River. Its banks are flanked with poplar and cottonwood trees. My house floated directly across a dike road from a working farmer's market. I knew the kids who needed Big Brothers lived mostly on the east side of town, far from the idyllic Sauvie Island life.

The Big Brother/Big Sister match specialist told me my Little Brother was living in foster care and he was an "at-risk" child. This governmental term was applied to any child who didn't live in a literate, two-parent, incarceration-free, drug-free, English-speaking, gainfully employed middle or upper-class household with three or fewer children. It is a definition applicable to almost half of the children in America.

As the appointment for the initial match meeting was scheduled, the support specialist told me that either the Big or Little could bail out if things didn't click.

"So—*you're saying he could dump me*?" I asked.

"Yes, he can dump you," replied the coordinator. "Pretty much anytime."

I wasn't sure I was ready for the possibility of being dumped by a kid.

I arrived five minutes late to the meeting. I nervously flung the office door open; it slammed against the wall. The receptionist escorted me back to meet with the match specialist. She stood outside the conference room, where Rico and his foster mother awaited me.

The match specialist explained how the meeting would go. I could see her lips were moving. I was so caught up in my own thoughts, about this kid I was going to meet, that I didn't hear anything she said. *Would he love the fact that we could make funny videos together? Would I have to teach him English? Was he happy or sad? Was he outgoing or shy?*

She finally opened the door to the conference room. There, at a large conference table, was Rico, a little Latino boy. He sat straight up, his hands neatly folded on the table in front of him. The large windows behind him framed a boulevard buzzing with cars. I took a seat across the table, near the door. A plump, smiling black woman sat next to Rico. She was his foster mother, Lorene—the adult who had signed Rico up for a mentor.

What Lorene knew about me was unclear. I was only told that Lorene and her husband James were Rico's foster parents. As part of our introduction, the match specialist asked us to share some personal information. "Rico, let's start with you," she said. "How about if you talk about some of the things you want to do?"

"I'd like to go hunting and fishing," he said in a monotone voice. With a slight inflection, he added, "I like football."

WTF? I hadn't mentioned *any* of those things in my application! In fact, I had deliberately omitted them. I inhaled deeply. *Remember. The Universe says this kid is for you.*

"Do you know anything about filmmaking, photography, music, or theatre?" I asked.

"No," said Rico.

"Would you like to?"

He stared at me blankly. "No."

I decided he would probably dump me.

We chatted a while longer. The match specialist smiled and interrupted us. She asked me to leave the room.

I leaned against a hallway wall and wondered how I could accept—or decline—a match based on five minutes in a conference room? *This was my chance to back out…*

I imagined myself saying "no thanks!" and leaving it to the match specialist to break the news. Rico would probably burst into tears and hate me forever. What kind of asshole would do that to a kid?

Time passed. I shifted from leg to leg and wondered what could take so long. If we were going to be matched, my biggest challenge would be satisfying Rico's wish to go hunting and fishing. *My dad was a hunter*, I thought. *He would love to take him hunting!* Then I remembered—dad was starting to go blind. Would my older brother Alan or my younger sister Denise take him? They both liked hunting and fishing.

They called me back into the conference room. Rico sat, staring down at a single sheet of dark blue paper. He was asked to read it aloud. It was an agreement like this one:

FRIENDSHIP AGREEMENT

- Matches are expected to meet 3-4 times per month and communicate by phone on weeks when they are not meeting in person.
- It is expected that the match will continue for a minimum of one year.
- The Big is responsible for obtaining prior approval from the parent/guardian for match outings and activities.
- The Big is responsible for arriving on time for outings and for returning the Little home by the time agreed upon, and the Little is responsible for being ready to go at the appointed time.
- Parents/guardians are encouraged not to cancel outings as a means of discipline.
- Bigs should not become involved in the discipline of the Little. The parent/guardian is the parent and the Big is the friend.

- Bigs are responsible for contacting the parent/guardian and the agency in case of accident, injury, medical or any safety concern while supervising the child.
- Bigs including other children in match outings, must obtain handwritten permission and a waiver of liability from the other child's parent/guardian.
- Parents or guardians may need to sign a waiver or permission slip with Big Brothers/Big Sisters to participate in any activity considered high risk or dangerous (horseback riding).
- The Big has no financial responsibilities toward the Little and his/her family or friends. The Big will be mindful of the parent/guardian's ability to pay for outings, and will try to choose free or low-cost activities.
- The exchange of gifts is allowed only for special occasions and should be simple and inexpensive.
- Bigs and Littles must wait to include family and friends in activities for the first three months.
- Overnight activities are not permitted until the match has been established for at least one year.
- The Big is not allowed to keep 'secrets' about the relationship, the young person or the family from the coordinator, even where the young person requests secrecy.
- The Little is not allowed to ask for money.

On July 24, 2006, Rico and I, with his foster mother Lorene, signed and dated our Friendship Agreement.

I was a little nervous, and wondered if this was what it felt like to have your first child. Did my 55-page training manual contain more rules and regulations than I'd face as a parent? I took a deep breath. *This is a one-year contract. If it doesn't work out, you can change your mind! A parent is stuck for life.*

Our first outing was scheduled to take place a couple of weeks later. The match specialist said she would check in regularly to see how things were going. In the meantime, she signed us up to get emails about free and low-cost events.

As I left the meeting, it dawned on me that I still knew nothing about Rico's parents—or how he ended up in foster care. Those details were, perhaps, left for Rico to relate. For the moment, it was helpful to learn more about his foster parents, James and Lorene. To this day, Rico still calls them Mom and Dad.

James, a welder in the Navy, had turned his skill into a successful career in the shipyards. Lorene had a long career as an office secretary before her back gave out. For the past several years she stayed home, raising foster children. Rico had been living with James and Lorene for over a year. He could be reunited with his birth family at any time.

Lorene was my primary contact, and she seemed to have a special fondness for Rico. Although James was an excellent male role model, Lorene knew Rico needed someone else to share activity time. Lorene and James had back problems that kept them from partaking in the kinds of excursions I would soon plan for Rico.

When I asked Lorene for permission to pick Rico up to go hiking at 7:30 AM on a Saturday, she replied, "Sure! That boy's like an old man—he's up every morning at seven o'clock!"

James and Lorene hade made an impressive emotional commitment to being foster parents. They lived with two—and sometimes three—foster boys in a modest two-bedroom, 1,000 square foot apartment in southeast Portland. The boys' room was stacked with three bunk beds, a desk, a couple of dressers and a closet. Rico had been there the longest of the children living with them at the time. The kids seemed to range from 10-15 years of age.

Over the next few years, foster children came and went in their household. James and Lorene asked to have one of their foster kids reassigned after he was caught shoplifting. Another was reunited with his mother, a recovering drug addict. Yet another boy became overly defiant and had to move.

It must have been depressing for Rico to see so many boys stay only a short time. He claimed he never befriended any of the other foster kids because he didn't like them. It made more sense that he couldn't handle the thought of befriending someone else who might disappear.

Discipline was important in a house full of young boys. Among the house rules was a requirement to read for two hours each day. After Rico was done with his daily reading, he had to write a one-paragraph summary and answer questions from James about what he'd read.

According to the Big Brothers/Big Sisters Friendship Agreement, Rico was expected to be home by an agreed-upon time. On the few occasions we returned late, Rico had to wait outside until James or Lorene let him in. They often went to bed early, and he had to knock on their bedroom window to wake them up.

I felt bad that, on more than one occasion, he had to sit outside for half an hour because of my running late. We both learned to make it a priority to be on time or to call ahead.

Rico complained about how hard James and Lorene were pushing him in school. When he did, Lorene would just laugh and say things like: "You better get good grades, boy, because you can't go running home to mama when you get out there in the world!"

Chapter 3

First Outing: Summer 2006

On a Saturday in August, I first picked up Rico in my shiny red Mazda Miata convertible. Summer mornings began early on the Sauvie Island houseboat. The mud swallows started singing outside the bedroom window about 5 AM.

In contrast, Rico awoke each morning to the sounds of trains and traffic outside his apartment complex. He lived in a subdivision consisting mostly of apartments, gas stations and fast food joints.

After leaving to pick up Rico, I passed by petroleum tank farms and marine industries, drove through Portland's urban core, and continued eastward another eight miles on Highway 84. When Mt. Hood rose in the distance, I got off the freeway, with another mile to go, through subdivisions of workforce housing.

After arriving, I entered James and Lorene's tidy apartment. The front door led directly to their living room, which was about 35 by 20 feet in size, and contained an overstuffed burgundy leather couch. In front of the couch was a glass-topped coffee table. Across the room from it sat an enormous television.

The apartment was usually dark, with the front curtains drawn. The TV was often on when I arrived. They watched *Judge Judy*, local news, and major league sports with the sound turned up loud.

On the opposite end of the couch, a small dining table was piled high with board games. Just beyond that was the kitchen and a sliding glass door that led outdoors to a cement patio where James and Lorene stepped out to smoke.

Rico and I spent our first afternoon together at a fundraiser for the Make-a-Wish Foundation. I wanted to make a lasting first impression, and remind Rico of something important—that there were always people in worse situations than our own.

My first mistake happened during that outing—right after we got into the car. I let Rico pick the music. *Never, ever let a teenager pick the music.* He changed the radio from jazz to rap. As soon as possible, I turned the radio down—or off completely, to lend an air of importance to my words.

"So—uh—what is it you want to be when you grow up?" *This was awkward.* He looked at me as if I had just killed his musical buzz.

"A doctor," he replied.

It turned out that "a doctor" was his stock response. It didn't matter who asked him—me, his foster parents, judges, counselors, therapists, teachers, coaches, or friends.

Several of my friends were doctors. It was a difficult path. I didn't want to discourage him, but thought that he perhaps didn't understand the high academic expectations. I understood why he might want to be a doctor, or any well-paid professional. My family was better off than Rico's, but we were hardly rich. In junior high, a poster on my bedroom wall reflected my dreams. It featured a man in formal attire, sitting in a Rolls Royce parked in a mansion's driveway. A butler stood waiting to serve him a cool beverage on a silver platter. The poster read: "My Tastes are Simple: I Like to Have the Best."

Compared to Rico, my childhood *was* rich—I had a bedroom of my own, which doubled as my father's den. Rico had a closet half-full of clothes and a bunk bed in a room he shared with two other boys.

"A doctor? Wow! Okay, what kind of doctor?"

"I dunno...What kind of doctors are there?"

Fellow Jews told me, years ago, that one of the best ways to respond to a question was to ask one in return. "Gosh. That's a tough question! How many parts of the body are there?"

Rico stared at me. Neither of us had a clue. "Well, however many there are," I said, "that's how many kinds of doctors there are!" Whenever I lacked an answer for Rico, I made things up. The real question would become this: *How soon will he know I don't have all the answers?*

We arrived at the fundraiser. Once we had our nametags, we ate and then played putt-putt golf. The course was set up on the second floor lawn of an expansive mezzanine patio at the offices of Blue Cross/Blue Shield in downtown Portland.

The festive atmosphere included white tents with appetizers, beverages and live music. A lawyer friend, Shawn Menashe, was one of the hosts. Shawn had invited us and was gracious to Rico. I was pretty sure Rico had never been to such an event before. He handled himself well, considering he was just 12 years old and we didn't really know each other.

For the big finale of the summer evening event, a Make-a-Wish child came out, head shaven, and talked about his dream to visit Disneyland. People made donations. We all hoped his wish would come true.

After our first outing, I felt a mixed sense of optimism and apprehension. Children were such wildcards. I'd seen friends and relatives struggle with them. Would this be my experience too?

At least he seemed like a clean kid. Since I'm pretty high strung, I knew that if Rico spilled cookies all over the floor of my immaculate Miata, it would take a lot of deep breaths to avoid losing my shit.

As I drove Rico home, I thought about the boy sitting next to me. What he was thinking as he went back to foster care? After seeing the Make-a-Wish kid dying of cancer, was he able to put his own life into perspective? Rico seemed well-adjusted and healthy. He was doing well in school. His life was full of promise and opportunity—after all, he had me, right?

For the rest of that first summer, we spent a few hours a week together. We played Frisbee in a hilly park and went biking on a trail near a runway of the Portland International Airport. For another outing, we drove an hour up the scenic Columbia River Gorge to hike among the waterfalls. We visited Oaks Amusement Park a few times, taking in the rides and enjoying the doughy goodness of deep-fried elephant ears in the crowds along the banks of the Willamette River.

One Saturday in September, I pulled into the parking lot of Rico's apartment building, turned off the ignition and stared at his front door. It was dark and raining; I wished I'd stayed home.

It had been an exhausting week. My parents' health was declining. At least once a month I traveled to Springfield to spend the weekend with them. We got along better than we had in years. But each visit was still stressful. Ugly memories surfaced every time I walked through their door. Coming to terms with their aging bodies and diminishing physical capacity forced me to consider my own immortality.

I was worn out emotionally and would rather have been aboard the houseboat, listening to the rain pounding on the metal roof. I wanted to curl up on the couch and watch TV.

Before long, Rico was in the car. The rain let up as we cruised along I-84 westbound toward Portland.

"Can I—can I—can I ask you a question?" he stuttered.

"Of course."

"Are you married?"

I gripped the steering wheel. My stomach churned with uncertainty. Seconds later, the clouds burst open; red brake lights flooded across the heavy traffic in all four lanes. I reached over to the radio and turned off his rap music. Though I was barely able to see out the window through the rain, I took my eyes off the road long enough to glance at him.

"Yes. I'm married,"

"Oh," he said, "What's your wife's name?"

Now he wants to know my wife's name?

I was being outed by a kid.

At about Rico's age, I first realized I was gay. His question made me uncomfortable. My thoughts flashed back to the time my father had ambushed me, and hosted a not-so-amicable coming out to my family.

Rico and I were supposed to spend the first three months getting to know each other *slowly*. I knew nothing at all about Rico's family. I didn't even know for sure that he had parents! I wasn't pressuring *him* for details. Why was he asking me this? I wanted to go by the accepted Big Brother/Big Sister rules. Why couldn't we just get together for ice cream and play Frisbee?

Rico was young. I hadn't had a chance to talk to his foster mother about how to handle questions related to his interest in girls and sex. Did he even know anything about sex? How could we talk about something so complex? I was afraid of having to manage his feelings on the issue; driving 60 mph on a rain-soaked freeway wasn't the best time to discuss it.

Older people were more predictable. Some work colleagues went years without ever discussing their private lives. Outside my circle of friends, I avoided more personal discussions. I rarely talked much about my weekends beyond the mundane, and steered clear of talking about relationships. After some emotionally bruising childhood experiences, I preferred less controversial subjects.

Our generation, of the 1960s and '70s, had far more complex issues surrounding being out than today's youth. Even so, this was not going to be easy.

I blurted everything out all at once: "Yes I'm married, but I'm not married to a woman, I'm married to a man. His name is David. We had a big reform Jewish wedding and then, a few months later, we got married legally in Canada, and then after that we got married in California." I took a deep breath. "Any questions?"

Rico sat quietly, and turned his head to stare out the window. He had been talking almost nonstop—until now. It was raining hard, and it was difficult to hear anything above the wipers' whip-thwak whip-thwak whip-thwak. My blood pressure steadily increased. Finally, he spoke.

"Oh," he said flatly. "Well, I'm still gonna call him your wife."

After I dropped Rico off at home, I sat in my car, buried my head in my hands, and cried. I already liked this kid. It was clear that he was going to change my life—how or why, I didn't know. Now that Rico knew I was gay, how did that make him feel? Did his foster parents not know? I racked my brain over what I might have said on my application, and in my interview. It was hard to remember—it had been so many months earlier.

I'd first learned about Big Brothers/Big Sisters at the Portland Gay Pride Festival. My sexuality didn't matter to the agency. Did it matter to his foster parents? What about his parents? What about him?

Our Friendship Agreement made it clear: we could be unmatched just as easily as we had been matched.

James and Lorene seemed to be fundamentalist Baptists. Rico had told me they made him go to church with them on Sundays. As a former Southern Baptist, I knew the church didn't exactly advocate for gay rights. At Trinity Baptist Church, in Springfield during my youth, we were told week after week that all gay people were going straight to Hell. I didn't want religion standing in the way of my friendship with Rico.

At home 45 minutes later, I was really stressed out. My life had been an act of quiet desperation to get people to like me. My heart and thoughts were racing. I forced myself to telephone Rico's house. Lorene answered.

"Uh, I just need to clarify a few things."

"Oh yes!" she exclaimed. "Rico was telling me about your wife!"

Oh my God—what?

"Well…I don't know what he's telling you," I said, "but I—I don't have a wife, I'm married to David."

"Oh yes, that's what he said," she said, giggling.

"I want to be clear. I hope that's not a problem?"

"No, that's fine," she said. "He's looking forward to seeing you next week."

What a relief!

Now came the issue of how to tell Rico more about my husband, Dr. Dave.

We'd met six years earlier, in February 2000. At the time we were both dating the same guy. Apparently, he didn't think it was going well with either of us. One day he said to me, "I'm seeing this other guy who's a real catch. It's not really going anywhere between us. I think you should look him up."

It was an unconventional introduction, but I appreciated his honesty, and searched out David's profile on gay.com. Our work schedules were so busy we couldn't find the time to meet. We played Scrabble, via the computer, for several weeks before we met in person. With each Scrabble move, we sent one another embedded text messages.

I learned David was a board-certified geriatric psychiatrist and chief health information officer at the Portland VA Medical Center. I asked him more questions about his career, and was totally surprised when he emailed me his 20-page Curriculum Vitae, complete with his date of birth and Social Security number.

As a former licensed private investigator and paralegal, I let him know he should never send such information to a complete stranger. It was clear that he was a trusting soul. I used the information to run a comprehensive background check. Within days, his report came back clean.

Soon, David invited me to his place for dinner. He served an elaborate homemade meal of vegetarian enchiladas and a trio of salsas made from scratch. He later mentioned that they were from a date he'd had the night before. I like to joke that on our first date he served me leftovers, but I still ended up with the whole enchilada.

David moved into my houseboat six months later. We lived there for seven years before we moved to a high-rise apartment downtown. We both walked to work. In true Portland fashion, we wanted to drive less to reduce our carbon footprint.

It was a relief to learn I was just being paranoid about Rico's foster parents. Lorene had made lots of gay friends while James was in the Navy and stationed in San Francisco. "They were so much fun!" she told me.

Rico asked me why I thought James and Lorene didn't like gay people. After my explanation that African-Americans tended to disapprove of gay men and lesbians, he became agitated and yelled, "That's so racist!"

Though I tried not to make racial assumptions, Rico was happy to point out my shortcomings. Like the Big Brother/Big Sister Training Manual said, my Little did not give me one inch of cultural credibility.

School started again for Rico. Before long it was football season. I got off work an hour early to watch him practice. I drove 45 minutes in the rain, through awful traffic, and stood outside in a steady drizzle for over an hour.

Out on the field, all the boys looked so tiny it was hard to spot Rico. The gridiron seemed to swallow them up. Lorene was there and she told me his jersey number. Although Rico had asked me to show up, and felt pretty sure he saw me standing there, he walked off the field without saying a word or even waving. It really pissed me off. *Was this how things were going to be for a whole year?*

Back home, it took me a while to calm down. I phoned Rico's house to explain that he hurt my feelings. Lorene answered and told me Rico was out with friends at Burgerville. I asked her to let Rico know that if he wanted me to get off work early and drive 45 minutes in the rain in rush-hour traffic—he would at least have to say hello. Lorene understood, and we chatted a while. After hearing my frustration about the fact that he wasn't opening up much emotionally, she let out a hearty laugh. "Oh, he loves you, he do! He looks forward to seeing you every week!"

After that, when I came to a game, Rico always said "hi" before he left the field. My hope was that he would talk to me like a real person—as if he were happy to see me there. But he was just a kid. Maybe it was too much to expect. He reminded me of my own childhood friends who were a bit clammed up.

If anyone could get Rico out of his shell, it would probably be my father. Dad had spent decades as an educator in the public school system.

Later that fall, I took Rico to meet my dad and mom. Getting older adults into his life, on a regular basis, might be good for him. James and Lorene weren't doing anything special for Thanksgiving, and Rico and I had been matched long enough for him to meet my family, so we drove two hours to my parents' house. We hadn't been matched for over a year, so we weren't allowed to have an overnight, and had to drive back the same day.

We had a nice visit, and after we said goodbye to my parents, Rico and were on our way to my car when he asked, "Did you tell them about me?"

The look on his face said what he really meant: *Did you tell them I'm living in foster care?*

I thought for a moment. "Yes," I said.

He seemed embarrassed, and a little disappointed. It dawned on me that he might have wanted to keep it a secret. It reminded me of the letdown I sensed from my best friend Russell when we were kids. I had a bad habit of over-sharing.

I felt awkward and embarrassed. "Your situation isn't anything to be ashamed of." As soon as those words came out of my mouth, I felt I'd blown the moment. Rico didn't need to be ashamed. He was just a kid.

Rico changed the subject; "my birthday's coming up you know."

"Oh yeah?" I asked.

We got in the car. "Uh, could I... could I... could I ask you a question?"

"Sure," I replied.

"There's this pair of shoes I really want. Do you think you could buy those for me?"

He was already angling for his birthday gift. His dream was to own a certain blue and white pair of Nike Air Jordans. A few days later, we went to the mall so he could try them on. Even though he wasn't yet 13, his feet were almost as big as mine. I bought the shoes, but told him he'd have to let me wrap them up as his birthday gift.

It felt strangely and unsettlingly paternal to buy him those shoes. Our relationship was supposed to be based on friendship and low-cost activities. Adding money into the equation changed the dynamics.

The Friendship Agreement said this without question.

At 44, I had barely figured out life for myself. Was it a risk to become some kid's father figure? Soon after buying the shoes, I got an idea to play a trick on Rico. He was such a serious little boy; he needed a little teasing—the way my brother would have needled me.

Back home, I replaced the Jordans with a pair of my old worn out dress shoes. After I gift-wrapped the old shoes in the Nike box, I put both pairs of shoes in the trunk.

A few weeks later, on his birthday, I took the gift box of my old shoes (and the sack with the Jordans) to James and Lorene's apartment. As Rico opened the box to find the wrinkled old shoes, his face froze in shock.

I piped up. "Don't you think what you really need are a pair of shoes for school, instead of those fancy old sneakers?"

Rico laughed nervously. His eyes cast downward. If he were heartbroken, he did a good job of hiding it.

I felt like a total jerk.

I grabbed the paper sack and handed it to him. He opened it, and smiled as he admired his new Jordans, I snapped some photos of him. To look at his face in those pictures, I realize how much they must have meant to him.

Rico's current home was the complete opposite of mine. My entire youth was spent in the same home. My parents still lived there.

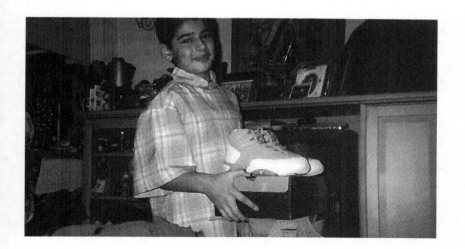

Chapter 4

Rewind: September 1962

When I was one-year-old and my brother was seven, my parents, Bob and Emily, moved to a new house. It was in a cul-de-sac in north Springfield and was part of a subdivision of single-level ranch homes with big lawns and manicured landscaping.

Our house sat a few miles south of the densely wooded Coburg Hills, and a quarter mile from the McKenzie River. It was a traditional flat-level house with three bedrooms and one-and-a-half baths. I shared a bedroom with my older brother. Our parents slept in a bedroom across the hall. When my little sister was born, a few months later, she was given a private room and a bed with a large, lacy canopy.

Our living room had a white stone hearth and fireplace, wood-paneled walls and built-in bookshelves. The shelves held a set of encyclopedias and numerous 17th-century ceramic figurines of women and children.

Small portraits of famous paintings like *Blue Boy* and *Pink Lady* hung beside several winged cherubs, which had been spray-painted gold. Our furniture was Ethan Allen's Early American. As years went by the furniture was only supplanted or recovered, never replaced.

The kitchen and dining areas were more casual. They showed my mother's southern roots. Her family moved to Oregon from Arkansas when she was a teenager. She had a soft spot in her heart for "mammy and pappy" salt and pepper sets. Dozens of hen-on-nest glass chickens sat, hatching mostly dust, on three shelves built into the bay window above the kitchen sink. Though she rarely drank tea, Mom had a display of fancy teacups in a small cabinet on the wall above our eight-track tape and music center.

Over the years she acquired boxes and boxes of decorations for all the major holidays: Valentine's Day, Easter, 4th of July, Halloween, Thanksgiving and Christmas—the ultimate extravaganza of celebratory crafting.

Our backyard was filled with plywood cut-outs of Disney characters, painted and nailed like little sacrifices to the redwood-stained fence. Bambi, Thumper and Snow White and the Seven Dwarfs surrounded our swing set and pink playhouse. A bell on the back porch called us home for dinner when we were outside with other kids in the neighborhood.

The backyard also had a lath house where Dad raised flowers for planting and hanging baskets. He considered himself quite the ladies' man and enjoyed sharing his homegrown roses with female co-workers, secretaries and office receptionists.

Our food budget was tight. Dad hunted for meat and mother scoured the newspapers for cents-off coupons. She and I went grocery shopping together on Saturdays and she always got the very best deals on Kraft Miracle Whip. In those days before bar codes, we often shopped at a store where we wrote listed prices on products with a grease pencil. Supposedly, not having to pay employees to label cans kept prices lower.

We shopped aisles of generic food products in packages with white labels and letters in thick Helvetica that boldly stated the contents: "BUTTER", "MILK", "MACARONI".

Our ranch house had a den and a two-car garage. Mom parked her car on the right side, next to the washer and dryer; the left side of the garage belonged to my father. Dad took care of the lawn mower, and his area held tons of built-in cabinets crammed with fishing equipment, hip waders, power tools, and other hardware saved, recycled and reused from years of scrimping.

He had rows of drawers stuffed full of nails, fasteners, screws, nuts, and bolts. He also had a large woodworking bench, skill saw, and power tools. His gear surrounded two upright refrigerators and a deep freeze packed with the victims of his hunting adventures (a deer he'd shot, fish he'd caught) and neatly packaged chunks of beef they bought to last through the coming winter.

Though Dad loved hunting and fishing, I refused to kill anything. When dragged along on his quests to catch or shoot an animal, I usually wandered off for a long walk in the woods. While meandering through the forest, I would sing Broadway show tunes to the trees and animals. One of my favorites was "I Talk to the Trees" from the musical *Paint Your Wagon*. Since it was all about singing to the trees and the wind, it felt weirdly normal and even somehow spiritual. I was a very theatrical child.

My brother Alan, six years older than me, enjoyed killing squirrels with a pellet gun. Since we lived a quarter mile from the ice-cold McKenzie River, he often stalked and killed the critters in our neighbors' hazelnut orchards. As proof of his conquests, he cut off their tails and pinned them to a bulletin board in our room. Alan had a number of collections—which ranged from stamps to mint-condition quarters. I was least fond of his dead butterflies, and the rows of hacked off squirrel tails.

Alan was a 170-pound, full-grown 17-year-old tackle football player. I was a twig compared to him. His idea of a good laugh was sitting on my face and farting, or giving me a wedgie. He reveled in his ability to belch, and could clear a room simply by removing his stinky socks.

Sharing a bed with Alan was difficult. Each morning, he was an immovable log. Mom and Dad had to throw water onto his face to wake him up.

One morning, when I was 11, I was jolted awake by a feeling of falling. The carpet was mere inches from my nose. I couldn't move my arms or legs. I had fallen over the edge of the bed, suspended by a sheet still tucked tightly under the mattress.

I hated my brother the bed-hog—and this was the last straw. I'm sure he didn't notice me falling off the bed as he rolled over and kicked me: I was a mere piece of driftwood on the seashores of his dreams.

Over the past year, I'd had a few sleepovers in the den at the other end of the house. With its hide-a-bed and large glass gun rack, it was not an ideal bedroom, but it had its own black and white TV. That morning, at age 11, I decided to move there permanently. I couldn't take another night of sharing the bed with Alan.

I pulled out my small dresser drawers and stacked them in the hallway. Dad emerged from his room and watched me. I was red-faced with courage. As I dragged the empty dresser past him, in my white JCPenney underwear, I screamed, "That's it! That's the last straw!"

My father chuckled, turned to my mother, and said, "Honey, your son is moving out, I guess."

I half expected my dad to stop me, but he never mentioned it again.

My brother grew older, crashed a few cars, and had several different girlfriends. One night, during an argument, my father got into a fistfight with Alan. I hid in my room, too scared to see what the argument was about.

For nearly the rest of my adolescence, I lived in my father's man cave. A glass-eyed deer head watched my every move. The gun that killed the deer was proudly displayed in that massive glass cabinet mounted above our upright grand piano. Life in a room filled with Winchesters and Remingtons should have given me the willies—but they were the least of my worries.

I had a lot of playmates in the neighborhood, but my best friend growing up was Russell. He was both a blessing and a paradox.

Chapter 5

Russell

Russell was the one friend I could count on to listen. His family went on skiing trips, while ours had campouts. They lived in a bigger house.

Russell was a tightly wound athlete and a vision of strength. He had a square jaw, big biceps, and large, dark brown eyes that widened with each smile or laugh.

We started first grade together and were classmates through graduation. We each lived about three blocks from our elementary and junior high schools, which were next to each other. By the time we got to high school, our dads worked together at the school: his as a guidance counselor, and mine as vice-principal.

Our junior high was named after Elias Briggs, a pioneer of Lane County. It was gray cinderblock painted even darker gray. Surrounded by a chain-link fence, and with almost no windows, it looked and felt like a prison. In the winter it was freezing. On warm days the halls filled with the aroma of teen sweat.

At the top of the unofficial student hierarchy, a tribe of jocks ruled over all manner of nerds and sub-nerds. In junior high I was a sub-nerd; Russell was a jock.

With six minutes between classes, hundreds of teenagers crammed the narrow halls in a mad dash. Sometimes, running was the only way to avoid being marked tardy.

Those six-minute breaks could prove treacherous. On a typical school day, I lugged a heavy stack of textbooks under my right arm as I clack-click-clacked down the cement hallway in my shiny two-tone patent leather shoes. I was fine until the sports jocks spotted me.

"Faggot!" one yelled, as he knocked my books to the floor. The echoes of his buddies' laughter rang in my ears. My homework flew out of my books and scattered across the hall, the pages stomped by the trampling hordes. On my knees, I scrambled to rescue my papers before the next class. On those days, my homework was decorated with footprints.

Russell was our junior high quarterback. He tried to protect me from the bullies. We had known each other so long he had a sort of brotherly affection for me. He had to have known I was gay, but in the '70s it was something you never talked about, even with your friends.

Though I didn't have words then for gayness, I knew I was attracted to men. I first realized it while out jogging; I caught myself staring at men's faces, which seemed more attractive to me. I was more nervous around men, and more drawn to them. Women felt more like friends. I didn't really have sexual feelings toward anyone until high school. I seemed to be experiencing the opposite of my male classmates.

Though Russell projected a tough guy image, at least twice in his life he told me he loved me. Not sexually, but deeply.

The first time happened when we went to live in the college dorms at Monmouth State College. It was for a program called Boys State, where we learned about politics and government. We created our own senate and legislature as student candidates ran for statewide offices.

We'd had a silly argument over one of Russell's girlfriends and something I said to her. As a result, I'd stopped talking to him. He came to my room and banged on the door. When I wouldn't answer, he yelled: "You know I love you buddy… but this makes it really hard for me."

I had no idea he loved me—not really. Like so many men, he assumed I knew. A couple of days later, we acted like nothing ever happened.

The second time was a few years after high school. He was floundering. He dropped out of college and was smoking a lot of dope. One night, while totally stoned out of his mind, he told me he loved me. We talked about what he was going to do with his life and a few weeks later he joined the army.

The best moments from our childhood friendship were the summers, when we spent nights in sleeping bags in our own backyards. They were nights filled with mystery. We stared at the stars and wondered where the universe began—and where it must end. We quietly whispered our thoughts and questions about the purpose of life and what happened when we died. In our wonderment of the galaxy we often scared each other with our deep thoughts and revelations.

"It must go on forever?" he'd ask.

"Well, if it has an end—doesn't that mean it's inside of something?" I'd ask back.

Inevitably, our discussions of the cosmos and extraterrestrials would end up back on Earth with licks in the face from Buffy, his golden retriever.

Not everything was unicorns and rainbows. Our personalities had different trajectories. I was nervous and shy; Russell was bold and outgoing, with an addictive personality. He started drinking alcohol early in life. While we were still in elementary school he would drink his parents' vodka and add water to what was left in the bottle.

By junior high he regularly snuck out of his house on weekends. He and his buddies went on destructive binges; they slashed tires and bashed neighborhood mailboxes with baseball bats. School buzzed with stories of their rampages—but he just laughed. He was a 4.0 student by day and a thrill-seeking vandal by night.

Russell sometimes treated me like a stranger, especially when he was with his jock friends. He tried to rectify it later by being extra nice. I could see he tried to straddle both worlds. To me it was good vs. bad, and it was a challenge to reconcile the two sides of his personality.

I reasoned with Russell to stop making mischief, but it did no good. I accepted him without judgment, and wanted to understand his contradictions. I hope he felt the same about me.

While still in high school, I met my first boyfriend, Mark. I had started performing in high school and local college musicals. We met after a show one night while I was dressed as a Jewish teen during a run of *Fiddler on the Roof.* Ironically, we were introduced by a woman who was playing Yentl, the matchmaker. Mark was a 27-year-old bartender and part-time student at the University of Oregon. He was the first man I met who liked me and didn't make fun of me.

With high school almost done, I still lived in my dad's man cave. Tapping at my window awoke me one night.

While I had been sneaking off at night to meet Mark, he had never been to my house. He usually picked me up a few blocks away. I couldn't figure out who was at the window.

My waterbed sloshed behind me as I cautiously approached the curtains, a familiar voice called out.

"Aaron?" asked Russell in a hush. "Let me in!"

Russell must have run away from home again. Maybe he was in some kind of trouble? Or maybe tonight he decided not to sleep in a neighborhood trash can or storm drain, as he sometimes did. I couldn't blame him.

I raced out through the back door of the garage, half expecting to find our snoopy neighbor lady staring over the fence as I rounded the corner to the backyard.

Russell sat on the patio, sobbing. We went back to my room and sat down on the waterbed. "What's the matter?" I asked. The bed sloshed as he clung to me. His shoulders heaved with grief.

I felt really awkward that night. *My* family didn't cry. I had no experience handling people's tears, aside from my own—alone in my room with the door closed, singing along with Karen Carpenter albums. During our 11 years of friendship Russell had never cried— or even *looked* like he might. He always seemed a tower of strength.

Over and over again he said: "My uncle...he killed himself. He's dead."

He had mentioned one uncle—a Hollywood film producer. As it turned out, he had another uncle who was gay. Russell seemed to feel close to him. Though this uncle lived far away, Russell blamed himself for not doing something to stop it. Looking back, I wonder if he felt he had been showing support for his uncle through me.

Our phone rang. It was Russell's parents. He didn't want to be alone, so they let him stay the night. I hope that I was of some comfort. I felt helpless—and totally clueless—about grief. I could only hope that my mostly silent presence was enough.

Only now is it clear how important our relationship was to me. It was so critical to my survival during adolescence that I invested in our friendship for decades.

Each of us could have done many things with our lives after graduation. Ultimately, my rejection by a conservative religion led me to spend another 30 years seeking religious and spiritual acceptance elsewhere. Russell ultimately gave in to darker impulses.

Of all my childhood friends, Rico would grow to remind me most of Russell.

Chapter 6

Year One:
January–May 2007

After the first round of holidays together, my meetings with Rico settled into a familiar routine. By spring, Rico was visiting our houseboat on occasion. We took many field trips out on the Island, including a hike to a remote lighthouse one dry winter's day.

Rico was disinclined toward exercising. This made our first run together (with David) especially memorable. The mid-March sky had cleared from a recent rain. It was about a quarter mile from our houseboat, down the wooden boardwalk up to the parking lot, and another mile and a half to 15-acre Wapato Park.

The park trail was a 3.2-mile loop around the lake. It was tough going for Rico, who trudged along pretty well until we reached the halfway point. Then he asked us to stop.

Rico had never done much running as far as I could tell. He wore the worst possible shoes. He'd declined my offer of new running shoes: they messed with his sense of fashion. We encouraged Rico to keep going, especially during the last mile. We ran way ahead of him on the road and called back to him, "Hurry up, old man!"

Since Rico was so much younger than us, David taunted him mercilessly.

I thought about how my relationship with Rico had changed. While most of our visits didn't involve other people, Rico seemed to really like David, who has a much different coaching style.

It was nice to have a part-time kid around. It was nice to feel like part of a family—even a non-traditional one. Rico had been surprisingly easy to get along with, so far.

Chapter 7

Year Two Begins: June 2007

Rico and I were about to reach our one-year anniversary. Was he worried that I would leave? I had felt many complex emotions as his mentor.

These days we were having pleasant times together, and he was even starting to grow on me a little. I was spending as much time with Rico as any of my adult friends—except David.

It was easy to feel protective of Rico, and to already be thinking of his future. I wondered if these feelings were usually only experienced by people who had a child. Seeing Rico every week was a big commitment, but it was hard to imagine telling him my year was up, and that I was leaving.

I had spent the past few years trying to tell my friends that I loved them. I wondered if maybe I should tell Rico. I *had* grown to love him, and it seemed important to say it out loud. His mother must have told him she loved him, but there didn't seem to be anyone else in his life who I thought might express those feelings. In my family, the only person who said I love you was my dad. He only said it to my mother, who had three stock replies: "Uh-huh," "I know that," and, "Yes, Bob."

Rico, I realized, had his own psychological and emotional vulnerabilities. He had never met his father, and had been raised almost exclusively by his mother and older sister.

Rico was still fairly distant from me emotionally. It took a lot of thought to decide how and when I should tell him I loved him. I didn't want it to feel weird, and hoped to express it in a natural, matter-of-fact way.

One day, as we left a lighting store, Rico stood on the sidewalk waiting for me to unlock the car door. It seemed that this particular space and time, with him separated from me by the car, yet still close enough to see and hear me, might be the moment to say the L-word.

I had the family curse of struggling (or neglecting) to express appreciation or emotion. Telling Rico my feelings required the delivery of a clear message, with a specific purpose, tinged with just the right air of fatherliness. I didn't want it to be creepy.

I rounded the back of the car. I stopped, stepped forward a couple of feet, and said: "You know I love you, don't you?"

"What?!" He leapt straight into the air.

I maintained my serious tone and nonchalantly opened my car door. I motioned for him to get in as well. As he sat down next to me, I stared transfixed on the steering wheel, saying, "Look, Rico, I just want you to know I love you." I turned toward him and continued in a serious voice: "I think it's important. When I was growing up, my dad never said it to me. He never told me even once. Not until I was over 40 years old!"

Rico paused to think. "Oh," he said. "And it would have meant a lot more when you were younger?"

"Yes, that's why. So I wanted to be sure I told you . . . at least once."

I didn't plan on telling this to Rico all that often, but if something happened to me, or if everything went dark forever, I wanted him to have heard me say it out loud.

Rico needed to feel he was lovable. He shouldn't be forced to spend years of his life as I had—engaging in happy self-talk, trying to get people to accept or like him. I didn't want him to be aloof like my dad.

Chapter 8

Year Two: July 2007

On our way downtown one day, I decided to tell Rico about my earliest memory.

"I was about four or five years old when our family was at the beach. I remember digging a hole in the sand. Dad was standing close by, and he asked me if I planned to dig a hole all the way to China. The tide started coming in and the waves washed onto my legs. The water knocked me face down into the hole. The waves rushed over me again and again and I imagined myself being sucked down through the Earth—all the way to China! I was certain I would die. I yelled: 'Help me! Help me, Daddy!' But my dad just stood there laughing. I was swallowing salt water and sand was going up my nose. He finally pulled me up by one of my flailing arms. Later I asked him, 'How come you didn't save me, Daddy? Why didn't you save me?'"

Almost 50 years later, completely out of the blue, my father recounted the same story. His version concluded with how funny it was—for him—to see my overreaction to falling into such a shallow hole. It was yet another reminder of the distance that existed between Dad and me for so many years.

"Dang!" Rico replied.

"Ok, tell me about your first memory."

"The first thing I remember," said Rico, "was when I was just a little kid, riding my bike on the sidewalk. When I turned my head to look around me, I ran straight into a telephone pole. My mom saw me and laughed. She said, 'That just shows how stupid you are!'"

That seemed harsh. I didn't know his mother yet, but it was a mean thing to say to a kid. All the same, my father and I had different reactions to a situation. His mother may remember his bike accident differently. What if, in reality, she had scooped him up in her arms, gently brushed his forehead with her fingertips and said, "that just shows how stupid you are," before she kissed his forehead? It's possible I wasn't getting the whole picture.

Since Rico had been talking to me about his feelings, I decided to ask a few questions. "So, Rico…what exactly happened with your dad?"

Rico was quiet for a minute, and then he said, "Mom told me my dad is somewhere in California. She doesn't know where."

"Oh. Have you ever met him?"

"No," he replied, squirming.

"I'm really sorry to hear that." It was sad to learn that Rico had never met his father. Despite my dad and I having had major disagreements (which often lasted for years at a time), it seemed that not having a father, period, was worse. In this quiet moment with Rico, I caught myself remembering things that had happened to me that weren't yet appropriate to discuss with him.

It was nice to feel that I could be there for him— even if that meant just sitting in silence. The closest thing I had to a Big Brother, at Rico's age, was a Young Life leader who taught me how to play tennis, drive a stick shift and pray to Jesus.

Rico and I were developing enough of an emotional connection to bridge any potential divide. Our silences were becoming less awkward: an acknowledgment that adding words didn't always add meaning. After learning Rico didn't know his father, it seemed more important to give him a sense of a normal family life—at least, as normal as it could be with a forty-something gay man in the picture.

There seemed no way to demonstrate the ups and downs of life than to show him that other people had plenty of their own drama. I was inspired to take Rico to see a play called *Holidazed*. The show, which I chose completely at random, turned out to be a little too much like Rico's real life. It was the story of foster care runaways who were taken in by a woman they met on the street. After she introduces the kids to her crazy family during the holidays, she ends up adopting them. As the story unfolded, Rico turned away and wiped his eyes, attempting to hide his tears.

The play had a happy ending. Perhaps it was the outcome he might want for his own life. I really wanted to talk to him about the play afterward, but it felt too raw. If nothing else, the play might help him understand that he was not the only kid who ever lived in foster care, or whose life seemed full of struggle. It might offer him a measure of hope.

The play was so powerful that the next day I wrote a note to the playwrights, Cynthia Whitcomb and Marc Acito.

Dear Cynthia and Marc:

I wanted to tell you that I went to see *Holidazed* not knowing what it was about, and I took my 13-year-old Little Brother with me from the Big Brother/Big Sister program. He has been in foster care for many years now. Although I have been seeing him almost every week for a couple of years, he has rarely opened up to me about his feelings, and it has only been recently that he has started to do that.

As soon as they started discussing foster care in the play I wasn't sure what we might be in for. He sat quietly next to me and in the touching climax of the second act I could tell he was weeping in the chair next to me, but since he is a teenage boy of course he covered it up pretty quickly. I like to think he left the theater that day with an appreciation of what it means to be surrounded by people who love you, even if they are not your real parents.

–Aaron

Later that summer, Rico wanted to see the movie *Game Plan*. Although he had no idea what the movie was about, he really liked its star, Dwayne "The Rock" Johnson. It turned out to be a heartwarming tale of an eight-year-old girl who shows up one day on The Rock's doorstep claiming to be his daughter. In her disarming manner, the little girl teaches the strapping pro football player about the rewards and importance of loving children and family.

Rico sniffled and wiped his eyes during the film's emotional high point. It was possible that he might have been thinking of his own father, and that if he could only find him, he would be able to teach him a thing or two about love.

We were talking one afternoon when out of the blue Rico asked me, "Did you notice my voice was changing?"

"Yes."

"You punk!" he exclaimed. "Why didn't you tell me?" While he had me laughing, he blurted out, "Will you be my Big Brother forever?"

I smiled at him, and felt my heart break a little. We had just finished my one-year commitment. I assumed we were operating more on a month-to-month basis.

It wasn't possible to know if David's job might take him to Washington D.C.—or whether I might need to move to Springfield to care for my aging parents. Rico might decide, in couple of years, that he didn't need or want me around anymore. There were so many unknowns.

I wanted to say, "I'll be your Big Brother forever," but that wasn't realistic. If I were supposed to teach him something about life, then he needed to know life was full of uncertainty and nothing lasts forever.

The diplomatic approach seemed best. It would give him the power to decide what happened, regardless of whether I stayed or moved away. "I'll be your Big Brother as long as you want me to. How does that sound?"

Rico missed having a dad. I had a dad growing up, but he hadn't liked me much until recently.

Chapter 9

My Dad Bob: Mayor of the Cul-de-sac

Dad was born in South Dakota to a poor farm couple during the Great Depression. He had two older sisters and a younger brother. He hated being poor and painted a vivid picture of a bleak childhood, where he was forced to endure brutal winters and searing summers. At age seven, he'd help his mom milk cows and then spend afternoons playing alone on an old rope swing in the dusty heat.

Although Dad managed to spend time with his father, he didn't like him. He often described my grandpa as a lazy, chain- smoking drunkard. He repeatedly told us that his dad made him sleep under the pool table at the local tavern while he drank.

Dad didn't like being left alone all day. He vowed, at a young age, that he would be a good father who provided for his children.

Throughout his life, Dad fought constantly with his two sisters. He referred to them as "selfish" and "lazy" almost as much as by their actual names. While he thought his sisters stingy, he criticized his younger brother for being too generous, and dismissed two of his brother's three kids as lazy, shiftless moochers.

My grandpa always talked so loud you could hear him a mile away. He had hearing aids, but refused to wear them. He was also a chain smoker, and put me and his other grandkids to work rolling cigarettes.

As a kid, it was fun to spend time outside on grandpa's cherry farm. It was pleasant there away from the yelling, and the smells of cigarettes and frying catfish. I mostly hung out playing in the mud around his man-made catfish lake.

I never really connected with my grandfather—I didn't talk very loud and he could never hear me. He would just yell "What?", "What?", "WHAT?" I didn't like having to yell to have a conversation. All the same, it was sad when he died at age 79 of emphysema.

I never met my paternal grandmother—she died of heart problems at a young age. The doctors said even though she was only about 50, she had the heart of a 90-year-old. Dad urged his mother to have surgery. When she died on the operating table, he felt responsible for the rest of his life. But because he disliked his father so much, he would often say his mother died of a broken heart.

Dad met Mom when he was 25 years old, and she was 23. They picked cherries together in an orchard for pennies a pound. One day, after they were done with work, Dad saw Mom standing alone in the rain under a tree, and offered her a ride home. Before long he proposed to her, and they were married. He got a job in a wood handle factory for a few years and worked there until he was drafted into the army.

After his military service, he went to the University of Oregon. He graduated with a degree in biology and began teaching. He later earned a Masters of Education and spent decades working in public schools. As vice principal at Thurston High School in the 1960s and '70s he was responsible for administering discipline. At that time it was a paid position, with job duties that included spanking students with a plywood paddle.

Dad didn't have much patience for kids who mouthed off, especially after he'd told them to get to class. An often-heard story around the dinner table concerned a student who made him so mad he picked him up by the neck and held him against the wall, nearly choking him to death. His frequent recounting of the event especially rattled me, since he stored his guns in my bedroom.

Another administrator saw the choking incident and pointed out he might be letting smart-mouth kids get the best of him. He realized his behavior was inappropriate and that he might find himself accused of assault and battery if he kept throttling the students. Dad asked the district to send him to anger management counseling, and they agreed.

The counseling seemed to help. He later used the choking story to explain that he could have gotten himself fired if he hadn't learned to control his anger. That he stopped choking students at work didn't always keep him from overreacting, but it definitely helped. His openness to reconsidering his behaviors and opinions continued to accelerate as he aged.

Guns were a staple of life in Springfield. Its citizens fought fiercely for gun rights. Dad's position on guns also evolved. A decade after he retired, there was a school shooting at Thurston High. In May 1998, Kip Kinkel took a Glock 19mm pistol and went on a shooting rampage. He left two students dead, and 25 others wounded, at the school my dad had worked at all those years. After supervising the school's administration, discipline and security there for two decades, he blamed its administrators as much as the gun-toting teenager.

"When I was there, I was wandering the halls every break and lunch hour," he said. "Those administrators just wanted to sit on their ass in their offices. They never got out talking to the students. They didn't know which ones were trouble and they weren't keeping an eye on them. I went to every dance and sporting event and concert to make sure someone was watching those kids."

The failure of security at the district, and the incredible tragedy of the shooting, had a major impact on his emotional state. Dad had worked with Kinkel's parents, Bill and Faith, who were both district teachers. Kinkel shot his parents dead just before driving to campus and opening fire on his classmates in the cafeteria.

On the brighter side, after 10 years of retirement, the kids on the neighborhood street were all calling Dad "Uncle Bob, Mayor of the cul-de-sac." Despite his fading vision, he seemed to know almost everything the neighbors were up to.

Keeping an eye on things in the cul-de-sac kept him busy. He had opinions on whether that single lady's boyfriend was good enough for her, or if the Mormon family's kids were being spoiled. He rarely kept these judgments to himself. His opinions about the neighbors were constant fodder for living room conversation. Whenever the opportunity arose, he'd let the neighbors know, firsthand, his thoughts on a wide range of matters—from their career choices to the best and only way to maintain a weed-free lawn—Dad's way.

"How are you going to keep supporting your family on that cabinet business, Brian?" he asked one neighbor. "Aren't most of your customers in California?" Because Brian's work often took him out of state, Dad thought he should stop that nonsense and apply for a maintenance job with the Springfield School District. My dad nagged Brian so often he finally applied for—and quickly got—the job.

With Brian, or anyone, Dad would launch into his favorite lecture on his theory of the social classes.

"We were all born in one of these classes," he'd say, ticking off his list:

"Lower-lower, upper-lower, lower-middle, upper-middle, lower-upper and upper-upper. Where do you fit?" He'd ask. "Everyone wants to say 'middle class.' *That's not right!* I came from the *upper-lower*. I wasn't a lower-lower, I was an *upper-lower*. I had to work my way up!"

After he explained his class types, he'd share his theory on the *only* four ways to change your social class. "You can marry for money, you can inherit money, you can develop a talent like Elvis Presley, or you can go to school and get an education. Those are the only four ways you can move up in society," he'd say. "I had to go the education route, and I knew it. I had a tough time but I worked for it."

By the time he reached age 70, when he wasn't presiding over the neighborhood goings-on, my dad took a weekly bus to Three Rivers Casino, where he spent the day playing the penny slots. He could still see well enough to sit and play his favorite machines for several hours. One day he even hit a $1,200 jackpot.

Dad became certain that history would repeat itself. He developed endless theories about the best machines to play and exactly when they would pay off. The slot machines became his new sport; he contemplated numerous strategies to improve his luck, much as he had done during all the years he fished for steelhead.

Listening to Dad recount his theory of the social classes made me feel like I was 12 years old again. This feeling brought back memories of what a disappointment I had been to him. I had tried sports because he forced me.

He took me duck hunting, deer hunting and fishing a few times. Though reeling in a fish could be entertaining and thrilling, I winced at the thought of bashing their heads before gleefully tossing them into an ice chest.

I didn't like touching dead things—especially having to slice their bellies open with a pocketknife and pull their guts out.

He once took me car camping when I was 12 years old. From the minute we arrived at the campsite, I begged to go home. He refused. I found a nearby fish ladder, and watched the fish swim upstream before I played in the river and walked alone in the woods. Two days later, he took pity on me; we went home. He never asked me to go fishing or hunting with him again. From then on he took my brother. If our entire family went, I entertained myself shooting a pellet gun at tin cans or wandering in the woods, catching lizards or poking at anthills.

For some reason, everyone seemed surprised when, at age 22, I became a life-long vegetarian and started following a guru.

Chapter 10

Year Two:
August 2007

The longer we knew each other, the more often Rico told me he wanted to be a doctor. Recently, he had gotten more specific—he said that he wanted to be a surgeon.

This seemed like a natural reason to take him to see *Body Worlds III: The Anatomical Exhibition of Real Human Bodies,* on display at the Oregon Museum of Science and Industry. Advertisements all over town boasted that the exhibit included over 23 full human bodies (and 200 body parts) drained of fluids and fully preserved in high-gloss, non-recyclable plastics.

It sounded so gross to me that I thought: *What pre-teen wouldn't love that?* I wanted him to see the muscles and organs of actual humans. He would need to know whether he could maintain the emotional distance required to be a surgeon.

The exhibit allowed us eerily close access. Many of the full-body exhibits were in "active, life-like poses" enclosed in glass. They were displayed as if living a somewhat creepy, strangely fulfilling skinless existence that included ice-skating, bike-riding and playing tennis.

We slowly ventured through the shiny petrified dead people. I tried to focus on the separate cases of individual organs, and read as much of the signage as possible to avoid any eye contact with the deceased. Rico bounded off ahead of me.

After about 10 minutes, I realized Rico had been gone for a while. I sped up trying to find him. Near a glass case, with a man clasping his own heart in his outstretched hands, Rico reappeared. He walked quickly past me to a wall in a dark, quiet corner. He pressed his back against it and bent over with his hands on his knees. He was directly behind a plasticized man holding his own skin folded up like a cozy blanket.

Rico was hyperventilating.

"Rico? Are you okay?"

"I just went to the abortion exhibit," he said.

"What? What did you do that for?"

"I don't know...saw it here before," he mumbled.

Rico seemed panicky. I could understand—just the idea of it grossed me out. "Okay...uh...so it looks like maybe you're ready to go? I mean, we can stay if you want...but we don't have to. It's okay if you want to go."

"Okay," he said quietly, without moving. He sure was rattled—God only knew why he wanted to see that exhibit again.

Chapter 11

Year Two: September 2007 (8th Grade)

After David and I moved downtown, we decided it didn't make sense to keep my 10-year-old Miata. We held onto the 2002 four-door polar white Saab that we had purchased new a few years earlier.

One Saturday after our move, we took Rico on a 4 to 5-mile-long urban hike. It was probably more walking than he had ever done.

During the hike, I had a truly parental moment.

As we neared the end of our walking route, we passed a GameStop. Rico begged and pleaded to look at some games for his Nintendo. We agreed to let him look. As expected, Rico soon asked if we would buy him several used cartridges. We had made it clear that he could just *look* that day. We tried to reserve the buying of such things as rewards for good behavior, or for meeting goals.

Rico hadn't done anything to deserve a new game recently, so our responses included: "Not now," "We'll think about that," and "We can talk about that later."

By the time we left the store, it was raining. We walked past a coffee shop and headed up a half-mile hill to our apartment. David was a fast walker; he took off in front of me as Rico sauntered behind.

At a stop sign, I turned around to make sure Rico wasn't lagging too far. He had completely disappeared. This shocked me. Was our relationship so fragile that he ran away the moment he didn't get what he wanted? I didn't know him well enough to be sure. We were two blocks from a MAX Light Rail stop. I imagined him hopping a train to get away.

Though I wondered if I were overreacting, my emotions were a blur. Nothing in Rico's past might make him run away, but something about him reminded me of Russell, who escaped from home dozens of times. Russell's life had not gone so well. I didn't want Rico running away from me or anyone else.

"David! Wait! I can't find Rico!"

"I'll get the car," David replied. "I'll meet you back at the coffee shop!"

Ugh. This could NOT be happening. How could Rico disrespect me like this? My palms sweated and my heart pounded as I retraced my steps. After a couple of blocks, something caught my eye. On some recessed stairs leading to an old craftsman house, Rico sat. Had he just been tired, and stopped to rest?

Since he was only 13, I tried not to swear. "WHAT ARE YOU DOING?"

"Nothing," he replied.

My eyes narrowed. I couldn't tell if he was tired and lingering, or pouting because he didn't get a video game. My emotions evolved from fright to fury. I loved this kid, and was responsible for him. I had never been responsible for a little person.

"Stop screwing around and get up!" I said.

As I continued walking downhill toward the coffee shop, he reluctantly fell in line. Two blocks later I checked back. He was gone. I assumed he had run off at high speed this time. Once again, he was discovered in a recessed stairwell.

This was maddening. Was it time to scream? Cry? I wanted to grab him by the ear and twist really hard, like my grandmother would have done.

"What do you think you're doing?" I asked, trying to maintain calm.

"I don't know."

This was a tough situation for me. Setting boundaries had always been a challenge, but I felt the need to command this relationship. However, I didn't want to become my dad. He had always told me exactly what to do. My knee-jerk reaction was to imitate his parenting style. A 13-year-old would not get the best of me.

I reminded myself that my year with him was up. Our contract was over.

In all our time together, Rico had never disobeyed me like this. It was a typical parental moment: kids do things that piss off their parents. I sure had. Rico probably had too. But now Rico was treating me like a parent. The difference was that a parent couldn't pack up and leave. But I could. I had no legal obligations. So I threatened him.

"You better knock this off!" I said, wagging my finger at him and speaking haltingly. "Because I am telling you RIGHT NOW that if you keep this up there is no way I am going to be your Big Brother. I AM NOT PUTTING UP WITH THIS. THAT'S IT!"

The color drained from his face. Overwhelming relief came to me for a split second. It was replaced by dread. Tears welled up in my eyes. *Maybe he was just testing whether it was OK to disappear from my life?* Despite my outburst, the thought of abandoning him was painful. "How do you think it makes me feel—having you disappear like that?" I demanded.

Tears welled up in Rico's eyes. I yanked him up off the stairs by the arm to make sure he stayed beside me as we walked the last two blocks to the coffee shop.

Patrons seated on an outdoor porch watched us as I pulled him up the stairs and held the door for him. I motioned for him to sit at a table by the window across from the counter. After we ordered something and sat down, it became clear other customers had taken heightened interest in our drama.

Being a disciplinarian didn't come naturally. It put me into my most uncomfortable emotional place.

Rico stared into his hot cocoa as my lecture continued. By this time David was waiting outside in the car. We drove Rico straight home.

It had been an exhausting day—and Rico never disappeared like that again.

Strangely, this feeling that Rico had been lost made me think about earlier times in my life when my parents had felt the same way.

Chapter 12

Rewind:
The Outing - January 1977

My parents' sense that I was an out-of-control teenager crystallized one unseasonably warm January night as Alan and I sat together in the living room watching *Portland Wrestling* on the black and white Zenith TV.

Dad strode into the room, and announced he was calling a family meeting. We had never had a family meeting before. "Did someone die?" I asked.

Denise, Mom, and my brother's wife Tammie filed into the living room and sat down.

Turning to me, my father said, "We've been having some problems with Aaron. Would you like to explain to everyone what is going on?"

Being called out and forced to talk was unusual—Dad liked to do most of the talking. But it was obvious what he was after. Though it was 1977, and I was only 16 years old, I blurted out, "I'm gay."

There were audible gasps. My 22-year-old brother started to cry. My sister's eyes got so wide I thought she would suck all the living room furniture into the black holes of her irises. My brother's wife Tammie sat calmly. Her gay brother, whom I had met, had probably told her about me years ago.

I figured my brother was crying because he was scared for me. If he had no problem killing things, why couldn't he handle having a gay brother? He usually acted so tough, but today he seemed like a real pussy.

They all acted so shocked and hurt. I wanted to stand up and shout at them all: "For God's sake, people! I've been gay since I was seven years old, singing along to Disney albums on my Close-N-Play in the backyard with Snow White and the Seven Plywood Dwarves! How can you pretend you didn't know?"

The so-called meeting couldn't have lasted more than an hour. It felt like forever, as various soundtracks and emotions rambled through my head on an endless train to nowhere. I was in such shock that many details about what else was said are a blur.

Dad made me tell everyone about Mark. He wanted to embarrass the truth out of me, because I hadn't told him everything he wanted to know. He seemed to think that if I were bullied enough, in front of everyone, I would relent. I simply reiterated what he had already been told: that I met Mark while performing in a local college musical, and that we'd been going out for a few months. I knew I was gay for a long time and was glad it was all out in the open.

There was an awkward silence. They stared at me, as if their hush might make me keep talking. I thought about how I must have looked, sitting on the couch directly under mom's gold spray-painted cherubs. To them, I was certainly no angel.

Their comments only made me feel bad.

"You're going to destroy this family," Dad complained. "What about our friends? They won't want to talk to us anymore. What will the neighbors think?"

Finally, at two minutes before midnight, exhausted from discussing my teenage sexuality, I stood up and proclaimed, "It will be midnight soon. Before the clock strikes twelve, I must return to my room—or I will turn into a pumpkin!"

I walked out on them and down the hall to my room. I locked the door. From the edge of my bed I stared blankly at the wall as the glass-eyed deer head gazed down upon me.

A few minutes later, my brother's wife Tammie knocked on the door. I assumed she was there as a friend—but she had been sent by my parents to keep me talking as they huddled outside my open bedroom window, eavesdropping.

I didn't say much: "I can't figure out why it's such a big deal to them, you know? I'm the gay one." My sexuality was obvious, and there wasn't anything to do about it. My parents seemed miserable, concerned about what the neighbors might think or what their friends would say. Did they worry at all about me? That really pissed me off. Was my sexual orientation the only standard of my worthiness as a human being?

Finally, everyone left me alone and I went to bed exhausted. I had to be at work by 7 AM at the *Springfield News* for my weekend job as a typesetter. As I struggled to fall asleep all I could think was: *Fuck them. I'm getting out of here tomorrow!*

The next morning, I spent every work break calling crisis hotlines trying to find out how soon I could be legally emancipated.

"I want to move out on my own," I told a woman at a legal hotline. "Isn't it possible to be emancipated? I turn 17 in a couple of months."

"It's possible, but it's a long process," she explained. "By the time you find an attorney and get through all the paperwork it could take a year."

Although I felt trapped and alone, there was nothing to do about it. I believed most of my relatives sympathized with me but said nothing. Perhaps they were afraid of incurring my father's wrath. If you got on his bad side, it could be almost unendurable— even if you didn't live with him.

A few months later, my 17th birthday arrived. I hung a calendar to count down the days until I was 18.

School started again. By then, my parents had deduced that they couldn't intimidate me into changing my sexuality; perhaps alternative measures were called for. My dad got hold of a creepy, dark film involving prisoners talking about being gang-raped. One evening, after a rehearsal for the school musical, he took me to a classroom where he had me watch the video. He stood at the back of the room, behind me, to make sure I was paying attention. It was unimaginably crude and traumatizing. I tried to blind myself to those awful scenes by closing my eyes.

This was exactly why I hadn't discussed my sexuality with my parents. They wouldn't just let it go. The ugly, disturbing film made me feel ashamed—and that I couldn't be loved.

A week or so later, I came home from school to find a book gift-wrapped on my bed. It was a paperback left by my mother. It had a picture of chains hanging on the front. The title was something ridiculously terrifying, like "Gay Bonds: The Links of Lust That Destroy Your Soul." It was mostly about how being gay had to lead directly to the fiery pits of Hell, since your soul was chained to pure evil.

A few months later, my parents ordered me into the Silver 442 Oldsmobile for a ride.

After passing through downtown Springfield, just a couple of miles from home, we turned onto a quiet tree-lined street along the Willamette River. We approached a cluster of low-slung professional buildings surrounded by oversized lawns and maple trees. We parked in front of one of the offices. It became clear they had brought me to see Dr. X, a psychiatrist.

We sat in Dr. X's dim waiting room. I began to doubt myself. *Perhaps I really could be straight and he knew some secret?* I was skeptical but perhaps I'd be surprised.

Soon after we entered his office, Doctor X called my name. My parents stayed in the waiting room. His office was also dark, with a single narrow vertical window. There was a banker's light on his hulking desk, and he ensconced himself in a cushy overstuffed leather chair, as I sat in a utilitarian version made of oak and gray pleather.

Though I could barely see his face, I noticed it was pockmarked. He was homely and seemed suited to the shadows.

"Do you know why you're here?" he asked.

"Well," I said, "I guess it must have something to do with the fighting that's been going on at our house lately."

"Yes," he said, "that's right." Then he told me a story. "I used to do a lot of hitchhiking back in my day, back in the '60s," he said. "I carried a baseball bat around with me to defend myself from those faggot truck drivers. A lot of those truck drivers are fags. They used to offer me a ride and try to get me to give them a blow job," he said. "And being a fag is just not normal. Are you a fag?"

Even at 17, it baffled me how this guy had ever received an M.D. in psychiatry. I had been reading the newspaper since I was 13, and knew the American Psychiatric Association had taken homosexuality off the official list of mental illnesses in 1974. It remained a controversy for many years, but it was officially settled. This guy was not going to learn about my private life. He was hostile and—what seemed even worse at the time—completely unattractive.

As far as I was concerned, he could sit here forever lurking in the dark with his pockmarked face staring out his narrow slit of a window onto his soggy-ass lawn.

I lied to his face. "I'm not a fag! But everyone thinks I am." Then I told him something true: "Every time I bring girls over to visit, my mom is a total bitch to them and they never want to come back."

The psychiatrist redirected his questions, asking something completely unexpected. "Do your parents ever fight in front of you?"

"No," I said. It was true.

"Would you bring more girls home if your mom wasn't so mean to them?" He asked.

"Yes! I absolutely would." That was also true. It might have been just to talk and tell stories, but I definitely would have had more girls over.

After about half an hour, Dr. X dismissed me from his office and asked to speak with my parents. My parents and I traded places. I heard my father raise his voice. Five minutes later, the door flew open and Dad stormed out with Mom right behind. I fell in line. We all got into the car and headed home. No one spoke a word.

No one said much at all for weeks until one Monday Dad woke me up early and said he was driving me to school. I followed him outside, where the pickup warmed up in the driveway. The morning air was cold and the cul- de-sac was silent except for the sound of the blurt-blurt-blurt of his poorly muffled white and mustard Chevy truck.

The cab was cold, as usual. Dad backed out of the driveway and headed towards the freeway. Most days he had his country music blaring. Today there was no radio.

It was scary when he was quiet. After all, he had guns and an explosive temper.

As we turned onto the freeway, he made a clicking sound with his lips, as if sucking on a toothpick. It brought to mind the small glass cowboy boot filled with toothpicks on our dining table, next to the salt and pepper shakers. Every night after dinner, Dad grabbed a toothpick and spent about 10 minutes chewing it as he picked meat and corn (or other vegetables) out of his teeth.

He shifted his body, which caused the vinyl car seat to scrunch. He stared straight ahead, without taking his eyes off the road and said, flatly, "I bet you think you're pretty smart."

We rumbled along the freeway past acres of green grass and evergreens. The smell of wood pulp, mixed with the scent of fall, filled my nostrils as we approached a perennial fog bank near the Weyerhaeuser pulp mill.

It was only a matter of time until I was free of him, and wouldn't have to listen to him telling me what to do anymore. I had to get through this and move on. For the first time in a long time I looked at him without fear. What had he asked me? *'I bet you think you're pretty smart?'*

"What?"

"You may have fooled that guy, but you don't fool me."

Sitting next to Dad in the truck that cold fall morning, I felt he had truly abandoned me. Perhaps I was not an ideal son, but I was on the honor roll, editor of the school paper, a singer in the jazz choir, and vice president of the thespian club! I had summer jobs every year such as picking beans, de-veining shrimp at a steak house, and working as the lot boy for Burkett Trailer Sales.

I could never be what he wanted: a hunter, a fisherman, or straight. The outside world might have imagined us the typical middle-class American family who had everything. The problem was this: like so many other families, we had everything except what mattered most.

Things between us stayed pretty much the same for the next twenty years—until I came home with a doctor.

Chapter 13

Mom & Dad Meet David: Summer 2000

At age 18, I left home as a strong-willed, independent teenager. I didn't speak to my parents at all for two years and mostly on holidays for 18 years after that. Our extended verbal exchanges took place at annual family gatherings and milestone birthdays. Before David came along, I'd brought a couple of boyfriends home to meet my parents. They didn't like either of them.

Each year, as I drove off from Mom and Dad's house after Thanksgiving or Christmas, I'd turn my head to see Mom standing in the driveway crying. To them, my life was a tragedy.

The day I drove with David to Springfield to meet them, they didn't know much about him—just that he was a doctor at the Portland VA Medical Center. Since Dad was a veteran, I hoped that might earn David some respect. It was always hard to guess Dad's reaction to anything.

It was the summer of 2000 when David and I headed up my parents' driveway together. My father opened the front door.

David spoke first. "Hi," he said. "I'm David. I hear you're a veteran! Did you know I can get you signed up so each of your prescriptions are just two bucks a month?"

The lure of cheap medications helped form an unimaginably strong bond. "Well, come on in!" said my father. "Would you like to spend the night?"

I couldn't believe the man standing in the doorway was my dad. *Had the body snatchers been here?*

On a later visit he took me aside. "I want you to know that I feel really sorry about how I treated you all those years."

I flashed back to some bad memories, took a deep breath, and imagined myself pushing them aside.

"It's okay, Dad."

He reached out and touched my arm, "No, it's not okay. I'm sorry."

My mouth dropped open. I'd never heard him apologize before. Somehow, Doctor David quickly found his way into my father's heart—a place reserved for a rare few. Before long, Dad told me how lucky I was to have David in my life.

Mom was a harder sell. The more David helped my father with his failing eyesight and VA benefits, the more she appreciated him. He was also able to track the state of her rheumatoid arthritis; within a few years she also told me how lucky I was.

On July 27, 2003, three years after my parents met David, we made history as the first gay couple married at Congregation Beth Israel. It is the largest reform synagogue in the region—founded before Oregon was even a state. It was a huge (and, no doubt, unusual) event, and it drew over 350 guests. My parents were even part of the wedding; Mom gave me away! It had taken a long time, but on that day there was finally a sense of unconditional love between us all.

It was the happiest day of my life.

Just a few years later, Rico would be celebrating one of the happiest days of his.

Chapter 14

Year Two: December 2007

The day he turned 14, I called Rico to sing "Happy Birthday."

"Are you having cake and ice cream tonight?" I asked.

"No, I'm not getting that this year," he said.

"What? Lorene's not making you a cake or anything?"

"No, not this year. There's just too much going on right now so close to Christmas."

Indeed, there was a lot going on, but since my parents had significantly changed their attitude over the past few years, I felt it would be good for Rico to spend more time with them. The older people in my life had made a real impression on me at his age, and since Mom and Dad were the closest thing Rico had to grandparents, we decided to take him along with us to see them that Christmas.

Before we left I picked up a double-layered chocolate cake, and as soon as we arrived, I covered it with candles while Rico wasn't looking. We surprised him with a round of "Happy Birthday."

"Thank you," he said quietly, giving me a hug.

It was Rico's second visit to my parents, and by that time, Dad was in his late 70s and fairly easy to take in small doses. His degenerating eyesight had forced him to stop driving, watching TV, and reading. About the only thing he enjoyed—besides sharing his wisdom—was listening to books on tape from Oregon's library for the blind.

Rico was especially excited about this Christmas visit. He'd been told about our ridiculously indulgent Christmases: a decorated tree, a stocking full of surprises, a dozen gifts, and breakfast with all the trimmings. He'd never had anything like it.

I wanted Rico to cash in. It felt like a great trade-off for the annual obligatory visit, which I'd skipped for a few years when we weren't speaking. These days I showed up out of guilt. Dad told me that my being there for the holidays "means a lot to your mother." It took time, but as the years passed, I started to forgive and love them again.

Rico soon realized that even Christmas presents had their price. He had to endure most of the same lectures I had heard for decades. It was difficult to hear them again without revisiting the emotional wounds of my childhood.

As Rico got his fill of Dad's stories and lectures on Christmas Eve, my sister Denise and her wife Lilly made comments about him. They had completely avoided both Rico and me. They left the room whenever we entered. David said, "They told me Rico slighted them last year at Thanksgiving."

"Oh? So that's why they're completely leaving the room when we enter?"

"They said they felt hoodwinked by the fact that you didn't let them know in advance Rico would be here. They would have rather stayed in a hotel. They think he smells bad."

If anything was smelling rotten in this family, it was negative attitudes. Since these complaints weren't made directly to me, I had no opportunity to explain. I could have told them that permission from my match coordinator to take Rico with us was given just one day before we left town.

It hadn't even crossed my mind that anyone felt entitled to special notice. I was starting to feel like Rico was part of my own immediate family. Certainly we were closer than my sister and I had been for many years.

After my gay outing in 1977, my sister spent decades as a Bible-thumping fundamentalist—telling anyone who would listen that I had destroyed our family. She was intolerant of other lifestyles—until, at age 40, she came out of the closet as a lesbian.

By this time, Dad had mellowed so much that my sister's announcement of her orientation barely registered. "Hell, *I* knew that!" he said, "I can't believe it took her so long to figure it out!"

Dad may not have known what took her so long, but I did: she was terrified by the way I was treated.

This nasty behavior had to stop. I told Rico: "We've got to do something to talk my sister off the ledge. Do you think you could say something tomorrow morning at breakfast, before we start eating? Dad usually asks who wants to say something, and if no one volunteers he'll launch into his own speech. That's your cue to jump in and thank everyone. Can you do that?"

"Okay," he said.

My intentions were to get through the day as politely as possible. David was angry with my sister because of her snide remarks. He thought Denise was unbelievably insensitive. She didn't understand the blessing of being able to help someone out. I hoped actions would speak louder than words. Perhaps her heart would soften with Rico's words at the breakfast table.

By the next morning, the dining table was expanded to seat eight. The dainty hand-crocheted white linen tablecloth was topped with shiny gold-plated flatware, special holiday plates and matching napkin holders. Each place setting had antique green glasses filled with sparkling red cranberry cider. Miniature ceramic snowmen held tiny signs in their puny arms with our names to indicate our place at the table.

Mom's Chihuahua hovered at our feet, hoping for fallen scraps as we took our seats and passed around that morning's bounty: scrambled eggs, hash browns, ham and buttermilk biscuits. There was oatmeal for David and me, the vegetarians.

As we took hands for the Morning Prayer, I worried about what Rico might say. I guessed It couldn't make things worse.

"Does anyone have anything they'd like to say?" asked Dad.

Rico spoke up, "Uh—can I—can I—can I say something?"

Dad turned to him with an encouraging smile. "Well, sure there, sonny boy!"

Rico cleared his throat, sat straight up and spoke clearly. "I just want to say that I really appreciate you all letting me be here and treating me so well."

My mother was always emotional on Christmas morning. With Dad's health in decline, her tears welled up whenever anyone expressed emotions.

"You are like a second family to me," said Rico. "These are the times I will always remember."

I was especially proud of Rico that day. It took courage to speak up like that. Although he thanked my family for their hospitality, they really hadn't treated him all that well. My mother put up with him; my sister thought he smelled; and my brother—well, he wasn't sure what to think.

My dad seemed the only one who enjoyed having Rico around. The more he learned about Rico, the more he seemed to be reminded of his own childhood. Dad understood that Rico was as poor as he had been as a boy, but also enjoyed watching the conflict between me and my sister, just as he appeared to relish his conflict with his own sisters as well.

In the end, Rico made off with some nice holiday gifts. It was a great excuse for David and me to buy him a bunch of things he needed.

Months later, I realized Rico had nothing to gain by speaking up that morning. He only did it because I asked him to. He wanted to show that he loved me. Somewhere along the way, our family lost the ability to appreciate how lucky we were. It took Rico to remind me.

Chapter 15

Year Two: January-Summer 2008

After the holidays, at the end of January, Rico landed on the school honor roll, with top grades in algebra, humanities, life sciences, PE, health, and drama. He'd told me a couple of times he was taking drama, and said he was doing well. Although he got an A, he said he wasn't going to take it again. Maybe the stigma of being in theatre was still the same—his friends probably accused him of being gay.

Rico's report cards had great comments: "Rico is a pleasure to have in class." It was easy to be proud of him. He gave me a bumper sticker proclaiming "My kid is on the honor roll." I pasted it on the sun visor inside my car so we could both remind ourselves of his success from time to time. Seeing him was much more fun when he was doing well in school.

Spring quickly came and went. We hung out together bowling, playing in video arcades, going to the zoo, visiting the science museum and hitting the gym.

During the summer, I ran across some pictures from his 12th birthday. Rico had changed the way he dressed. Gone were the starched men's short-sleeve dress shirts worn loosely hanging out of his pants.

When I saw him later, I asked, "Why did you stop dressing like that? Except for the baggy pants, I liked the way you looked in those shirts."

"Because," he replied, matter-of-factly, "that's how you dress if you want to be in a gang."

I made a mental note: *ask to have a section added to the Big Brother/Big Sister Training Manual: "Tips to Help Your Little Stay Out of Gangs."*

When it was time for back-to-school shopping, Rico asked to go to a low-rent strip mall where fashions included baseball caps, t-shirts, saggy jeans, hoodies and various brands of sneakers. I had never heard of the place. When we walked in, it was pretty clear why: there were two dozen black men, Rico, and me. It was the kind of scene I hadn't run into much in Portland, which is sometimes mocked as *Whitelandia.*

Rico requested a $70 pair of torn jeans. He didn't want to try them on before I bought them, but I made him do it anyway. We had already returned clothes a couple of times because they didn't fit. As soon as Rico walked out of the dressing room to show me, we argued.

Me: "Those are hanging down under your ass!"

Rico: (pulling them up six inches) "No. These are OK."

I was reminded of the bell-bottom pants I had worn as a teen in 1978. Nothing could dissuade him. Only time itself would embarrass Rico in full measure.

He held up a black belt covered in white spikes. "This would help me keep them up!"

I didn't like the jeans, or the belt, but arguing was pointless. *So what if he wanted some ripped jeans?*

"Okay, you can have them."

"I love you, brother!" he exclaimed.

"What?"

I'd been seeing Rico for over two years. He had never said he loved me before. I wasn't sure how to react. I stared at him, trying to figure out whether he really meant it—or if he was just grateful to have some new clothes. Wouldn't it take more than baggy pants and a hideous belt? I wasn't offering him much in terms of emotional support—he kept mostly to himself.

Watching him cling to those jeans made me realize we had something else in common: we loved clothes.

While my tastes ran to blazers, sweaters, Polos, dress shirts and Italian pants, Rico was partial to baggy, saggy pants, backward baseball caps, and Nike Air Jordans.

This was how our clothes fetishes compared: For $250 I could buy a pair of limited edition Persol sunglasses (handmade in Italy), a Brooks Brothers SaxXon wool blazer (from rare sheep shorn in Australia) or a Scottish cashmere sweater. While I loved owning any of those things, Rico preferred to spend his money on a pair of high tops made in China. It was a generational difference.

Later, Rico texted me a photo of some shoes and shirts, and asked me for fashion advice.

Me: "I am shocked you want to know what I think!"

Rico: "Well, it's been PROVEN that GAY ppl know there [sic] stuff lol."

Rico's desire for limited edition shoes inspired his first entrepreneurial experiences. He was one of those kids you saw on the news waiting in line for shoes that could immediately be resold—at $100 profit—to a kid at school. Sometimes, if he stored them away for a while, their prices doubled. By his mid-teenage years, he was making some decent pocket change.

Before the end of the summer, Rico asked me to help him transfer to attend Lincoln High, also known as the rich kids' high school. It was on the west side, near our apartment. He claimed he would get a better education there than at Parkrose, where there were more low-income students. I wanted to help.

Changing schools meant Rico would need to take public transit for about two hours a day. He said he was willing. In order for his transfer to succeed, an application had to be filed about a year in advance.

The paperwork had a long trail: Students who wanted to transfer districts had to get approval from their current school before they applied to the school they wanted to attend. The receiving district also had to approve the transfer.

I learned that school districts have quotas on the number of students they allow to transfer to other schools. Any school district that gives up a student also had to surrender their state funding for that student. To allow a child the freedom to choose was like giving away cash. Dad had taught me that no district was in a hurry to cut its own budget. No doubt the lengthy application and approval process was created to deter as many transfers as possible.

Child Protective Services was in favor of Rico's transfer. Even so, the districts weren't interested in waiving paperwork deadlines. After untold hours spent trying to decipher the whole frustrating process, I considered letting Rico use my address as his home, which would have defaulted him into the district he wanted. He had asked if he could do that, but I feared someone would eventually figure out he didn't actually live with us, which would have led to still more paperwork.

As we slogged through the transfer discussions, Rico finally began to talk to me about his family. He told me he had a sister, Gabriela, who was two years older, and a brother, Luis, who was seven years younger. Each had different fathers.

While the two boys were born in the U.S., Gabriela came across the border, at age two, with her mother.

Rico and his siblings were taken away from their mother after officials felt one of the children was being abused. Because child protective services felt Rico's mother knew—or should have known—what was happening, they intervened. After a police investigation, the alleged perpetrator fled the country, and Rico's world was soon blown apart.

Rico's mother denied knowing about it. Whether she knew or not, as an undocumented immigrant she had valid personal reasons to fear any police spotlight on her family. Deportations were on the upswing. Illegal immigration was a hot news topic. Rico would fear his mother being deported for many years to come.

After a formal court hearing, Rico, Gabriela and Luis became wards of the state. The court cases for Rico and Luis were separated from Gabriela's, presumably because she was not a U.S. citizen and quite a bit older. The children were sent to foster homes around town, miles apart. The state allowed Rico to have occasional supervised visits with his mother, brother and sister. And though Rico loved James and Lorene, he longed to be reunited with his family.

When he finally told me more details, I couldn't believe how long he kept all this stuffed inside. How awful that must have been—being dragged off at age 11 to foster care. How did a removal to foster care go down? Did the police—or some kind of guards—come to the house and take him away? Did they pick him up at school? Where did they talk about what was happening? Was it at the police station? Juvenile court? How much detail did he get about the process? What was it like meeting his foster parents for the first time?

It took Rico two years to open up to me. If there was a sense of unease between us, perhaps it came from his inability to trust me enough to expose his vulnerability. I might finally be starting to reach him, but it wasn't clear how to give him a sense of security.

I wanted to ask more detailed questions, but decided they'd have to wait.

Chapter 16

Year Three: Fall 2008 (9th Grade)

By the beginning of our third year together, Rico was beginning his high school freshman year. The court case that started when Rico was 11 years old was still going on at age 14. For three years, the state had employed a raft of professionals who, in theory, worked together to serve the needs of each family member.

By this time, I'd already been in contact with Rico's caseworker for two years. She invited me to what would be the first of three court hearings I'd attend. At the first, the court made a decision as to whether Rico could move back in with his mother on a trial basis.

I saw Rico's mother, Maria, for the first time outside the courtroom. She was in her mid-40s, about 5'4", stocky, strong, and—as my father would surely have noted—big-breasted. She wore a clean, pleasant dress; her long black hair was pulled back in a tight ponytail. She wore glasses and was lightly made up. Like the majority of women of Central America, she did not wear nylons or shave her legs. I later learned that her hairy appearance was a constant embarrassment for Rico.

As a gay middle-aged white guy, I couldn't imagine what it was like living in America as an undocumented Latina. It was hard enough being gay. Hiding under the radar, undocumented, and having your kids in foster care would have been a major blow. Although I was suspicious of her, I appreciated that each of us was part of a group that others despised: undocumented Latinos were blamed for stealing jobs while gay people were tagged by some as the culprit behind AIDS and global warming.

I introduced myself. Looking a little worried, Maria thanked me politely for helping her son. In her broken English, she said that Rico needed a male role model in his life. I didn't really know anything about her, and felt a little guilty for thinking that Rico should stay in foster care. She seemed to want to have him live with her, but his academics deserved priority over family until he was out of high school. I rationalized my support for foster care based on conversations with Rico's caseworker Cindy and his therapist Veronica. It was hard to imagine how his mother would be able to provide an environment that allowed him to focus on his education.

The court hearing involved the cases of Rico and his seven-year-old brother Luis. Both had lawyers present. After entering the courtroom, Rico's mother sat with her lawyer on one side and translator on the other. I sat in the audience with Rico's therapist, while Rico was seated parallel to his mother, at the opposite side of the courtroom, with his attorney and caseworker by his side.

There were 11 people in the courtroom related to the case. The only people not being paid were the boys, Maria and me.

When it came time for introductions, the judge thanked me for working with Rico. After the judge had heard from all parties involved, he asked if anyone else had anything to say. I stood up. "Your honor, I have been Rico's Big Brother for almost three years and I would like to say that I don't think it would be in his best interest to be moved to his mother's home until after high school graduation."

"And why is that?" asked the judge.

"Rico's grades have been getting worse. He needs the structure offered by his foster parents. If he moves back in with his mother, he'll be able to do whatever he wants, without enough supervision. I don't know about you, but I would have loved that when I was fifteen years old. That wouldn't have been good for me and I don't think it will be good for Rico."

Rico stared straight ahead, as if he were oblivious to my words. I wondered what he must be thinking. I hoped he knew I was being honest about what seemed best for him. Before foster care, Rico didn't have much stability.

When the judge asked Rico what he had to say, he stood up and said: "I want to live with my mother."

"What about those grades?" the judge asked. "If you move in with your mom, are your grades going to keep going down—or are you going to work to get them back up?"

Rico promised he would work to improve them.

"You keep telling me you want to be a doctor," she lectured, "and you will never reach that goal with bad grades." She encouraged him to try harder, and to listen to the adults who were trying so hard to help. He agreed.

The judge requested the attorneys join her in her chambers for a private conference. When she returned to the courtroom, she announced she was awarding temporary custody of Rico to his mother. Temporary custody meant the case would continue while the court evaluated his progress and integration with his mother. I was disappointed.

A couple of weeks later, Rico moved in with his mom, who was pregnant with another child (a boy she would later name Diego). For several weeks after Rico's move, I didn't hear from him. He stopped responding to my voicemails and text messages. I waited three weeks, and then emailed my match specialist. Had Rico decided not to see me anymore? Was he pissed at me for what I'd said in court?

Dear Ellen:

I realize that as Rico gets older he may not need/ want to see me as often. The past three years I have tried to spend time with him almost every week. He is growing up quickly now. For all I know, now that he's living with his mother, he's expected to be the man of the house and get a job to help pay the rent. I don't have his mother's phone number. She doesn't speak English well. I am not sure how she feels about the Big Brother/Big Sister program.

My biggest concern is that he is living in the middle
of gang country where there is a lot of drug/gang/
prostitution activity, and a higher chance he could
be attracted to that kind of behavior. I don't like to
think so, because he is a good kid and I get a sense
that he is offended at kids who steal things (three
of his foster brothers were moved after they were
caught stealing). . .but I am concerned about possible
drug and alcohol use now as it will be more easily
accessible to him. . .obviously I am concerned and
hope to mentor him in such a way that this can be
avoided.

Does there ever come a time when someone needs
a different kind of big brother? I wonder that too. I
think he will miss having his foster dad in his life,
whether he admits it or not. It must be hard to grow
up without a father.

—Aaron

My match coordinator said she would try to find out why Rico had
not been in touch. She and Rico's therapist soon reported that he had
been working hard on his homework and trying to do better in school.
Had he really been so focused he forgot all about me? It seemed more
likely to me that he felt hurt and was retaliating.

Rico called me soon after, about something completely out of the
blue. "Hi," he said sheepishly. "I lost my winter coat."

"How did you do that?"

"I don't know. I packed it up when I left my foster parents and now I can't find it," he said. "Do you think you could please buy me a new one?"

"It's almost summer."

"I know!" He said, his voice rising. "But I'm gonna need one when school starts!"

I often fought against buying Rico things outside of birthdays or holidays. It was discouraged by Big Brothers/Big Sisters. But he was my Little Brother. He needed a coat—how could I not buy my Little Brother a coat?

The first time I saw Rico at his mother's apartment shocked me. Having been raised in a 1960s ranch house where cheerful gold cherubs and *Blue Boy* adorned the flat-white walls, it was difficult to appreciate the freedom that material things enjoyed at Maria's.

It wasn't especially dirty—just disorganized. The stacks and random chaos made me feel claustrophobic. Sometimes the floors were dirty; sometimes they were clean. Sometimes food sat on the counter. I wondered how the family kept from getting sick. I tried to accept things the way they were, but couldn't help wiping the counter or throwing out the trash. I made it a point not to criticize Rico's mother, and to remind him how hard she worked to keep the family afloat.

Rico never had a room to himself until his last few months of high school, after his sister moved out. Most of the time Rico was at his mother's, he slept on the living room couch. He kept almost all his things in the coat closet by the front door. The closet held his neatly organized boxes of clothes, and Nike Air Jordans stacked in their original boxes. His skills at organizing seemed more out of necessity than desire. Anything outside the closet might be sucked into the vortex of the hurricane where it could be lost for months on end.

At the close of Rico's sophomore year, he had mostly B and C grades. Though that was disappointing, I would soon long for the days of C average grades.

During one visit, Rico asked, "Can we go camping this summer?"

"Uh—no," I replied. "We won't be taking you anywhere alone for a while."

"Why not?" he asked.

"Let me explain. How do you think it would look to people if two middle-aged gay guys took a 15-year-old boy camping overnight alone?"

He thought for a minute. "Ohhhhhhh," he said.

"Exactly. I would love to be able to do that, but it's not time yet. I'm not being judged the same way a straight Big Brother might be. So we will only be taking you somewhere where there are other people around. Okay?"

"Okay. So, can you take me to Hooters?"

"I am not taking you to Hooters, no." I could just imagine the newspaper headline: "Big Brother Takes Minor to Hooters."

Chapter 17

Maria

When I first met Rico's mother in 2008, she spoke in halting English. Most of what I knew about Maria came from her two sisters and her daughter Gabriela, who are more fluent.

Born in Guatemala, Maria grew up in a rural Mayan family during the country's genocidal civil war that raged from 1960 to 1996. Maria entered the US illegally in 1992, after escaping Guatemala by way of Belize and Mexico.

Several years after Maria's arrival in the United States, President Bill Clinton acknowledged that the U.S. government had supported the Guatemalan security forces that had committed human rights abuses during the war. Those abuses included the torture, kidnapping and murder of thousands of rural Mayans.

Guatemala's leaders were eventually convicted on charges of government-sponsored genocide. The damage done totaled more than one million displaced natives, including more than 830,000 Mayans.

During the war's early years, Maria's mother was kidnapped and held prisoner as a sex slave. She bore four girls and a son—some the offspring of her kidnapper. After Maria's mother escaped and returned to her village, she opened a bakery to support her family.

Maria attended school through the second grade. She didn't like going to school. She had trouble paying attention and remembering things. Her mother let her drop out and put her to work in the bakery and at home, helping to raise her younger brother and sister. After their mother died of cancer, the bakery was burned down by rebels. Maria's oldest sister fled to the U.S., and eventually found her way to Oregon.

After leaving Guatemala, Maria became pregnant and gave birth to Gabriela. When Gabriela was two years old, Maria hired a "coyote" to lead her into the U.S. so she could be near her oldest sister. After she arrived, Maria's youngest sister soon followed.

Maria's unauthorized entry into the U.S., after escaping a civil war ironically funded in part by U.S. taxpayers, was made worse by the fact that she had smuggled in Gabriela. From the time they were young, Gabriela and Rico were taught to fear drawing the attention of authorities, which might result in the involvement of immigration officials.

Maria could read some Spanish, but she couldn't write it. She didn't read or write English, although she could understand simple concepts and, with some struggle, speak in halting phrases to explain what she wanted.

Gabriela learned Spanish as a child. As she grew older, she talked to her mother more in English, unless she needed to translate. Rico knew Spanish at a beginning level but opted to communicate almost exclusively in English with everyone, including his mom. As Rico grew older, when he was forced to speak to his mother in Spanish, he tended to yell in his attempt to get her to understand.

Maria spoke Spanish fast and fluently. Her modeling of speaking rapidly collided with her young sons' inability to speak English at the same pace. As a result, they suffered from patterns of stuttering. This was most pronounced in Rico.

It was a fitting metaphor for their love. They struggled for years to find a way to communicate. Maria had sometimes jokingly called her son stupid. By the time he was a teenager, in anger he called her stupid to her face. The fact was—like many boys and their mothers—they had a lot in common. Like it or not, Rico was his mother's son. Her challenges would become his for decades to come.

As time passed, I grew to appreciate Maria's many positive aspects. But at first it was hard to comprehend why everyone in court constantly referred to her as "delayed". The answer presented itself soon enough. For the first two years of our acquaintance, she referred to me as Eric, Rick, Darren, and by several other names. At first it seemed like a joke, but I soon realized that she literally could not remember my name.

Rico found it embarrassing. "Ma! His name is Aaron! How many times do I have to tell you?"

Chapter 18

Year Three: Summer 2009

Rico was a sophomore when he asked David and I to hire Maria to clean our house. As a federal employee, David was subject to the headaches of an IRS investigation; hiring an undocumented worker wasn't an option for us. Aside from the legal issues, it was uncomfortable to think of Rico's mother folding my underwear. After all, she couldn't even remember my name!

Rico was really worried, as his mother had to leave a few recent jobs to avoid being detected. This seemed like a good time for Maria to consult an immigration attorney. I had worked with a good immigration lawyer a few years earlier, and made an appointment for Maria to see her.

Maria learned about possible future options for naturalization, but didn't take action at that time. None of this news went to my Big Brother/Big Sister match specialist. My involvement with my Little Brother's parental naturalization would have been frowned upon. It could be interpreted as my having too close a relationship with his mother.

Despite his family's poverty, Rico dreamed of joining the Black Friday hordes at Lloyd Center Mall, and asked me for cash to buy his family Christmas gifts. After much thought, I gave him $120 with a caveat: he had to show me receipts for everything. David constantly warned me that *any* cash was enough for Rico to buy drugs.

A few days after Black Friday I asked Rico, "So what did you get your family for Christmas?"

"Oh, I didn't buy anything,"

"You didn't? So you still have the money?"

"No. Not all of it. I spent twenty dollars at Wal-Mart and ten dollars on a party."

"OK," I replied, "Well, since I'm your Big Brother, I can't give you money for parties. That wasn't our agreement, so you need to give that money back to me." To my surprise, he opened his wallet and handed me $90 in cash.

It was disappointing that he had lied to me, and gone to a party instead of Christmas shopping like he claimed. I worried he might go off the rails, as Russell had done. I took a deep breath and sighed. As I stuck the cash back into my wallet, memory overtook me.

In the years since our childhood, Russell had gone through rehab and served two separate sentences in the state penitentiary for felony convictions. His first conviction was for armed robbery of a corner grocery—probably while high on crack. He was released a few years later, but it wasn't long before his addictions caught up with him. He was back in prison for auto theft.

Did I fail to give Russell the emotional support he deserved from me? Could anything have been done to keep his life from spinning out of control? In an attempt to make up for this lack of attention, I wrote to him in prison occasionally and sent holiday gift baskets through a pre-approved vendor.

Months went by. I kept a close eye on Rico and continued to worry about his behavior. It seemed he had stopped listening to me. I wrote Russell to ask for a favor.

Monday, July 19, 2009

Dear Russell,

I have this feeling of déjà vu. I'm having nightmares about this little brother I have been working with Rico for 3 years through the Big Brother Big Sister Program. He's a tough little guy and in the last year has grown really fast. He's almost taller than me.

As a big brother, I have been spending time with him almost every week since June of 2006. We have done a huge variety of things and I have tried to be there for him. He's been tough to get through to emotionally. The first year or so he didn't really talk about his feelings or anything, and he was willing to do that for about a year, but now I feel like I am losing him, which I guess is somewhat to be expected in adolescence.

At ongoing monthly hearings at Child Protective Services he insisted he wanted to move back with his mother. Now that the Judge finally put him back with her, I am pretty sure she will not be nearly as strict as his foster parents. He is basically a good kid but I think that now he is living with his mother he will just run all over her and stay out all night partying. I am not going to mince words here so I hope you will forgive me if I offend you in any way. What I would really like you to do is to do me a huge favor and write him a letter about the things you might have done differently in your life if you had it to do all over again.

Rico does know something about you already. I told him about you a long time ago. He knows how much I love you and feel like I always did whatever I could to help you, but somehow that just never worked out to be enough. Even years later he sometimes mentions you to me out of the blue.

I guess it's a good thing I have you to write to because I had a dream two nights ago that Rico was doing meth or crack or something; then when I called him yesterday (after he declined to go on a hike with us) he said he had been out late partying and that he was going to a party again on Saturday afternoon. It was the way he laughed and kind of sneered when he said it that made me feel even more freaked out.

Here is this 15½ year old kid who is basically a ward of the state, he is probably going to parties and drinking and getting stoned. I need you to help me. He's smart kid but I think I might lose him because his caseworker is overloaded and you know how a teenager can get away with a lot (we could in the old days and it's worse now!)

I think I can help him get a part-time job in a few months, so it's really just this time period between now and then I'm worried about.

You don't have to tell him everything I said. If you could just tell him that you know he has a good future ahead of him if he can stay focused on his sports and school and stay out of trouble... and that you are writing because you have heard so much about him from me that you wanted to write and tell him he should listen to me when I tell him stuff. That would be awesome. You can help me try to make a difference in his life.

Thanks man.

Love, Aaron.

I got a quick response:

Dear Aaron:

I was so glad to get your letter with pictures and info about Rico. I guess we're all at that point in our life when we wonder what its all about and what kind of impact did we leave. I'd like to hear more about your goings on. I wrote Rico (letter enclosed), I hope it plants a seed. I can't even get my own kids to write. I feel sorry for myself and think they just don't want much to do with me. But Mom and Dad do a good job of reminding me what I was about at that age. God Aaron, 50 is around the corner—guess it's time to wake up?!

It's been great writing with high school friends. It has really helped me with stroke recovery. I wish I had the choice to not remember the bad stuff, but unfortunately it doesn't work that way. Just the fact that I'm writing somewhat legibly is a miracle compared to 10 months ago.

I'd like to say I've had some radical insight, some paradigm shift—but mostly I'm standing, staring, wondering blankly what the answer is - then realizing I've forgotten the question. So I continue on kind of blankly tripping in the cosmos of time - wondering, what's next?

I'm busy enough, writing letters, playing music,
reading the Word, walking 5+ miles every day.
I've been here about 5 months now. Still have yet
to get a 2-man room. Dorms suck! Thank you for
the money. As I am sure you are aware they keep
80% so if by God's grace you should ever desire to
send more please don't send more than ten dollars
at a time (they don't take anything from that.) I was
taking college course in "information technology"
but it appears budget crunches are going to end that.
It's gonna be a long couple of years! Aargg. I'm at
Monroe by choice to hopefully get some medical
benefits (tooth repair, heart maintenance, Hep C
Treatment) but so far all I've received is a pair of
glasses. I shouldn't bitch, it is nice to see—I'd not
realized how blind I've become.

Would love to hear about your life or just "shoot the
shit." God bless you bro.

Love, Russell.

Russell had meant so much to me. I imagined Rico in his shoes
35 years in the future. I feared receiving a letter from Rico on my
deathbed, saying he was 50 years old and in jail.

Russell struggled to find meaning in his life from the time we had
been teenagers. His dad pushed him hard to be a better athlete. Russell
was powerful and fast but it wasn't his dream. Much like Rico, he
acted tough on the outside, but was actually quite sensitive. Russell's
dad made him feel inadequate, paving the way for him to turn to
alcohol and drugs to escape.

I held Russell's separate sealed envelope addressed to Rico. I had no idea how timely his letter would be.

August, 2009

My telephone rang. It was Lorene, Rico's foster mother.

"Rico stopped by here for a visit today," she said, "and he has something he wants to talk to you about." The phone changed hands.

"Hi," said Rico. His voice was quiet and serious, and it reminded me of Russell.

"What's up?"

"I got into trouble. I wanted you to hear it from me first," he said.

I waited for him to continue.

"I was caught shoplifting," he said.

"WHAT? What did you take?"

"Pokémon cards."

I lost it. "I JUST BOUGHT YOU SOME OF THOSE FUCKING CARDS!"

"I know."

I tried to sound calm. "Did you *really* need more?"

"I know. I'm sorry."

My mind raced—I might be a Big Brother, but at that point I felt just like a parent, and I hated it. What did Rico need—a good listener, or someone to tell him to get his act together? What would help him more: acting like a brother or a father? What was the difference?

"I could understand if you were starving and needed to eat something. But you aren't starving." I lowered my voice and tried to sound dispassionately factual. "Well...are they taking you to jail? Are you in jail *now*?"

"Nooooooo!" He protested, adding nervously, "I didn't get charged."

I had spent five years working at a city courthouse and knew a little about shoplifting violations. Rico's situation was complicated: he was still a ward of the state, since his mother did not have full custody. Part of me hoped they had handcuffed him and taken him to jail to scare him a little.

My deepest fear was Rico's failure in life. It seemed such an eerie coincidence that the letter to Rico from Russell had arrived a few days earlier. I wondered whether my attempt at prevention was wasted.

We had plans to get together the following day, so I told him: "I'll talk to you about it more tomorrow."

The next morning I called. "I think we should go for a drive today."

"My mom wants me to go to the beach with her and my sister," said Rico.

I wasn't surprised that his mother wanted to visit with him, but it seemed strange they'd planned a trip to the beach the day after his shoplifting episode. In fact, I had thought of taking him to the beach, to get him away from his normal environment so we could have a serious talk.

I told Rico we could see his family at the shore, and he agreed to ride with me. From their house, it was two hours to the coast. It was a beautiful day to drive through the coastal mountains, and neither of us said much.

By the time we got to the beach it was drizzling rain with a bone-chilling wind. I popped the trunk to get a picnic basket packed with falafel sandwiches, carrots, hummus, and the letter from Russell.

With Rico and the wicker basket by my side, I strode into the fog and sat on a bench. Rico sat next to me as dozens of gulls called out and misty rain blew sand straight into our faces. The ocean roared in the distance.

"What did your mom say about your shoplifting?"

"She said—she said—" he paused, and fought back tears—"She said she was disappointed in me."

I offered him a sandwich. He refused.

"That food's gay," he said.

"Shut up and eat, Rico," I said. "Here, this letter came for you a couple of days ago. It's from my friend Russell, who's in jail. I asked him to write you because I'm starting to feel afraid that you'll end up in jail like him. I want you to read it out loud to me."

Rico looked at the front of the letter with his name handwritten across the front. He turned it over and ran his fingers across the words: **"THIS WAS MAILED BY AN OFFENDER CONFINED IN A WASHINGTON STATE CORRECTIONS FACILITY, ITS CONTENTS ARE UNCENSORED."**

"Is this real?" he asked.

"Yes."

Rico opened the letter.

"Read it to me," I said, "out loud."

After an initial introduction, Rico read:

> ...partying is what teenagers do—it's what I did. It's
> what I thought everybody did—so I thought. The
> reality was that myth allowed me to keep on getting
> blitzed. I lost my share of friends growing up—not
> just lost—but dead, you know—last shot, one more
> hit—all that jazz. You young men today are all too
> familiar with it through the music, movies, videos.
> If it's not that you're too different to die, it's that
> you don't care. If it's meant to be it will be. Believe
> me, there's really very little we truly have control
> over. That's why it's so vitally important we take
> advantage of every opportunity presented us.

I guess one thing I'd like you to consider is this: Party time has been around seemingly forever—long before you and I, and long after we're gone. I don't know man, maybe you're not partying every chance you get. Maybe just a little weed now and then— and then all of a sudden, boom you're sitting on a T bunk eating top-ramen burritos at the age of fifty. Like I said, I'm not here to "scare straight" anyone, you've probably seen more shit in your young life than I'll ever see. If you hear anything—please hear this: You've got someone who is willing to offer opportunity (something that not many have) stop feeding yourself bullshit that you don't care, or that there's no tomorrow, or that you're not good enough, or maybe you're too good?

I don't know bud, I've had more opportunity than most. I partied my way out of two college scholarships, four marriages, high paying jobs, lost opportunities—was it worth it? Dumb question—I am blessed—I've been offered one more shot. I'll get out of here in a few years and maybe, just maybe have one more shot. No one is guaranteed tomorrow. That's partly why I stopped everything to write this letter. If this is my last night, I realize that the party got me nothing. And if one thing I can share might cause someone to at least pause and think about the next move.

Don't be like me (definitely) and not a 'mini-me.' Life is way too short for party time all night, day, week, month, year—Please please take a moment, take a breath and pray for an answer. You don't necessarily even have to ask a question. Shake your head, open your mind up, and an answer for your next move will be given.

There's not too many people I can say that I truly respect, but Aaron is one of them. We may not see eye-to-eye on everything, but I do know this—I wouldn't be writing if it weren't abundantly clear how he feels about you.

They say that grace is an undeserved gift; an opportunity—we just gotta step forward and take it.

I hope something I wrote maybe at least caused a little 'pause for thought.' It's up to you, not society, not your circumstances, no one but you—step forward towards becoming a man—and I guarantee your life will become better than any you ever dreamed possible. And the party will still be there at the end.

Peace to you bro—write back if you like.

With God's love,

–Russell.

I sobbed as he read it. It brought back so many memories and shattered dreams—so much unfulfilled promise. Russell had lost four marriages, but his first was the longest. He had fathered two children who were like strangers to him today.

Like a true Jewish parent, I squeaked, "End up like that and it will destroy me!"

Rico blended the myriad roles and relationships I'd had in my life. I had been that son whose father thought he was out of control. I had lost a best friend to a series of bad choices. Thought I empathized with Rico's need to rebel, I began to understand a father's sense of desperation. How could I use these experiences in a way that might support Rico as a Big Brother, a father, or a friend? If he stopped trusting me, listening, or otherwise shut me out—as I had done with my parents—was that the end?

We stood up and walked through the tiny beachfront town of Seaside, toward the beach where Maria, Gabriela, and Rico's 8-year-old brother Luis would be waiting. I tried to tell Rico that he meant a lot to me, but couldn't get the words out without crying. I didn't want to look at him. I didn't want him to see me break down. The sadness in his young life was getting to me. I was afraid I might not stop. And after all, my family didn't cry.

Finally I said, haltingly: "I don't know what I would do without you."

We met up with Rico's family. His sister Gabriela, never shy about expressing herself, immediately yelled out. "Rico needs a male role model! He's misbehaving. He's talking back to Mom!"

It felt like she was accusing me of failure. As her rant continued, it was easier to shut out her noise and examine her facial expressions. Her words washed over me like waves crashing to shore. Her lovely face contorted as anger raged forth.

"He has anger management issues!" she exclaimed. "He punched a hole in the wall in the living room while he was arguing with Mom and now he's stealing!"

As she vented to me, Rico stood with his head down and stared at the sand. He looked like the quiet, sad little boy from when we'd first met.

His mother regularly confessed to me that Rico left her feeling helpless. But how much could I help? I was just a volunteer.

Gabriela's rant was exhausting. I told Rico it was time to keep driving down the coast. We headed a few miles south to Cannon Beach. The sky suddenly cleared and the sun glittered on the ocean. It was a welcome reminder of how much beauty there is in the world.

"Wow, this weather is sure a lot nicer than in Seaside. And it's just a few miles away." I felt hopeful that the day might shape up more as I had imagined earlier.

Rico turned to me and halfheartedly said: "All the Latinos are in Seaside. This town is whitewashed."

He was right, but it wasn't beautiful because the town was whitewashed. It was beautiful because the *weather was nicer.* Rico seemed to see the world through the lens of race. He was more worried about fitting in than creating a life of his own. I had experienced both sides of that coin. How could he learn to see—or create—those opportunities?

~   ~   ~

After the shoplifting incident, it seemed that Rico could not focus on his schoolwork and sports without being in foster care. I contemplated calling the State to report his shoplifting. It seemed like something in accordance with my Friendship Agreement paperwork. Rico's mother wasn't his full legal custodian yet, and she knew about his theft, but the State didn't. That seemed to put the state—his legal steward—at a disadvantage. I called DHS the next day.

When I reached a State employee, I said, "he just moved back in with his mom last month and he's already staying out all night and shoplifting."

She flatly replied: "Unless the child is being physically or verbally abused by the parent, there's really nothing we can do."

That didn't satisfy me. I called and emailed Rico's juvenile caseworker, Cindy.

A couple hours later, Rico sent me a text: "Call me after work."

Me: "What's up?"

Rico: "It's important."

I called that evening.

"Would you do something for me?" he asked.

"What's that?"

"Could you not say anything about the stuff my sister talked about at the beach, and that I went there with you? The caseworker might think my mom is being too easy on me. They might put me back in foster care."

"Look, if someone from the state calls me up, and wants me to talk about what is going on with you, I have to tell them what I know. I'm going to tell the truth."

There was an uncomfortable silence. I tried to better communicate my feelings. "In this situation, you are the one with all the power. You have the ability to make choices, and your choices have consequences. I can't make decisions for you. You're going to have to live with whatever happens." I had already reported everything, but I didn't feel like explaining it all right then. I probably should have.

A few days later Rico texted me: "Did you tell my caseworker anything?"

Me: "Yes, I did, so stop worrying about what I said about things and start telling the truth."

Rico: "It's just that she told someone I got arrested. I wasn't put in handcuffs or a police car." Apparently he had been detained and released with a warning.

Me: "I may have said you were 'picked up for shoplifting' but parsing words is like trying to put lipstick on a pig. Shoplifting is a pig and a pig with lipstick is still a pig."

I wrote to our Big Brother/Big sister match support specialist about the incident. She replied:

Hi Aaron,

Thank you for keeping me in the loop about what's going on with Rico. Your communication with his case worker is the best course of action I could ever recommend. I'm really impressed with your honesty and pro-active attitude. I'm also glad that Rico doesn't seem to be upset that you shared details of his shoplifting. There may be consequences for his behavior with the judge, but it's a natural side effect of breaking the law and it's a good (but unfortunate) lesson to be learned.

I understand the past few weeks have been really frustrating for you. Rico is dealing with a lot of new challenges in his life and you're really trying to guide him through it. Help Rico focus on what his strengths are and how those traits will help him carve out a better life for himself. When things seem like they are at their worst, just remember that patience, consistency, and friendship are your strongest allies.

Thank you again for being a caring Big Brother!

−Ellen Z.

Apparently something was lost in translation in my prior email to Ellen. Rico was *very* upset that I'd told anyone about his shoplifting.

In the end, no charges were filed against Rico for shoplifting. When he appeared at his next juvenile court proceeding, the judge was displeased. In an attempt to lighten her mood, Rico told her he was thinking about joining the Navy after high school. The judge made a point of telling him that he couldn't have a criminal history if he really wanted to enlist.

One morning, not long after, I woke up and immediately started to cry. I don't know if I had been dreaming, but an overwhelming sense of grief, sadness, and fear came over me. I feared Rico might be lost. I pictured my mother thinking of me. *Is this how she had felt?*

David was still asleep next to me. I tried to stifle my sobs. I rolled over on my side and stared out the windows toward the glow of the sunrise on Mt. Hood, 90 miles to the east. David reached out and touched my back.

"What's wrong?" he asked.

"I'm not sure I can handle this."

"Handle what? What is it?"

"Rico," I said, as tears streamed down my cheeks.

David put his hand on my shoulder. "Honey, your dad and I were talking about Rico. You know that you're not his father. He thought maybe you should let him go. He's not your son. It's been three years. That's a long time. You aren't responsible for him. You can sign up for another Little Brother… you can find one who will appreciate you."

As soon as he said those words, I felt a brief sense of calm. I wanted to let go *so badly*. But this sense of peace was crushed by a sudden, impending feeling of dread. The thought of saying goodbye to Rico was somehow much worse.

"I can't do it… I can't be another adult who gives up on him."

David hugged me close. "It's OK," he said, "That's why we all love you. I'll do whatever I can to help. Everything will be all right."

Chapter 19

Year Three: Escape

In the aftermath of Rico's shoplifting incident, I felt that David and I needed to hold some kind of intervention to separate him from his friends. I wanted to get him outside his neighborhood for a while. We made plenty of time for Rico that summer.

In August, Rico had his first plane ride on our trip to Indiana and Kentucky. Our first stop was Anderson, Indiana, for David's 30th high school reunion. It seemed like a great opportunity to expose Rico to America's calmer, conservative heartland.

In Anderson, Indiana, Rico met two of David's three sisters, his mother and her (fifth) husband, several nieces and nephews and many of David's oldest friends. Sadly, Rico's exposure to small-town life in the Midwest wasn't the uncorrupted experience I'd imagined. Among other things, the reunion was a veritable showcase of alcohol abuse, and rumors swirled about former classmates smoking pot in the parking lot. It seemed that for some of David's peers, things hadn't changed much since the '70s.

We conspired to keep Rico occupied with guest registration and event clean-up, both during and after the party. At one point, midway through the evening, I escorted Rico outside for a chat. We sat in our rental car and watched people hanging around the entrance to the event hall.

"Is this what happens to everyone after high school?" he asked.

"To be honest, this is pretty much what it will look like at your 30th reunion. You have to look around and figure out which one of these people you want to be when you grow up."

"Oh, wow," he replied.

We sat quietly for the next hour and took in the wide variety of people around us. The crowd in the parking lot smoked cigarettes and drank, as inside the hall we knew others were dancing and carrying on. Every now and then, someone emerged to wander off. The entire experience was a little weird.

On our way back to our hotel that night, David and Rico and I had a long talk about the life situations of certain people he had met. We worked hard to make it a "this is your life" kind of moment.

The next morning, before we left Indiana for Kentucky, David drove us further into the country, along a single-lane gravel road that he had traveled often during his childhood. We neared an old wooden shack surrounded by weeds, a dead tree, and a rusted-out Chevrolet Impala. David stopped the car. He was silent for a moment, and then wistfully said, "There it is—the house where I grew up."

"Dang! That place is trash!" Rico exclaimed. In comparison, Rico's apartment was nicer, so he felt comfortable talking smack about David's childhood home.

"My older sister Lisa and I lived there with my dad after the court decided we were better off with him than our crazy mother," said David. "Dad worked the night shift at General Motors. Even though Lisa was seven and I was only five, we usually spent the night in the house alone after he tucked us in for the night."

"Wow!" I interrupted, "Your dad would be charged with child neglect for that these days!"

"Yeah, I suppose so," said David. "My parents' divorce was so unusual that psychology students from the local college sat in and wrote papers about their psychological warfare."

"That's messed up," said Rico.

David and his three sisters had all done exceptionally well in life after a childhood filled with major difficulties. David's sister Lisa became a rock singer, and later settled down with a man who had been a big fan of hers. Rico never said anything, but it was obvious he was impressed by David's grit. David often pointed out that his background was very much like Rico's, and that life was what you made of it.

The next stop on our road trip was Dunbar, Kentucky, where Lisa lived with her husband on a 1,600-acre cattle ranch. I had wanted to visit the Bluegrass State ever since I wrote a paper about it in junior high. Kentucky was beautiful, green, and exceptionally hot.

We made the most of our time on the ranch where Lisa's family raised thoroughbred racehorses and cattle. The barn had several four-wheelers, and we rode them all over the ranch's gravel roads and hundreds of acres of grassy, rolling hills. One day we used them to assist with a big cattle drive led by Lisa's son, Drew, who was just a year older than Rico.

As I watched Rico riding around on the four-wheelers, it was hard to believe it had already been three years since we signed our Friendship Agreement.

It had taken a long time, but Rico was finally able to go fishing like he'd always wanted. He also got to ride horses and drive a car on miles of empty gravel country roads. The only other time Rico had driven was one Christmas at my parents', when he backed the car into the corner of an old cinder block supermarket and crushed a rear corner taillight.

After the fact, I realized I probably needed to get a waiver for Rico to ride a horse. And I'm sure it was a violation for him to drive a car.

For a moment, paperwork was forgotten.

Early in the morning, a couple days later, after a quick stop at Cabela's to get Rico some hiking boots, we visited Mammoth Caves National Park. The Ranger had us all sign the requisite liability release forms, and then led us on a four-hour caving expedition.

Our excursion included about a half hour in caves where we stood up, amazed at the giant black enormous caverns. Then we spent another three hours in tiny, confining tubes that required crouching or crawling on our hands and knees to pass through. Anyone with claustrophobia should avoid caving at all costs. As I dragged myself through a tiny tube, hundreds of feet underground, I had to focus on deep breathing to avoid being overcome with a sense of panic.

When we were done I asked, "So, Rico... what did you think of that?"

"It was interesting," he said.

"Do you want to come back sometime and do the six-hour version?" *Please dear God don't let him say yes.*

"Nah, I don't think so," he said. "That was hella scary a couple of times."

Rico especially enjoyed spending time with David's nephew, Drew. Drew had become a three-time Junior Olympic gold medalist in Taekwondo. Later on, in his early twenties, Drew became a top student and leader of the second battalion at the Citadel military academy in Charleston, North Carolina.

I was sad when it was time to say goodbye. Rico had been well-behaved while surrounded by David's relatives, and seemed like a different person. Perhaps he acted the way he was expected to among a family full of achievers.

Later that month I turned 48. For my birthday, David took Rico and I to dinner with another gay couple. I'm sure it was the first time Rico had been out with four gay men at once. After the waiter served our entrées, my 60-something friend Bill peppered Rico with tough questions.

"So what do your friends think about you having a gay Big Brother?"

"Oh, they don't think about it," said Rico.

"Really?" asked Bill. "They didn't notice anything and ask you about it? What do you tell them about David and Aaron?"

"Before my friends meet him, I just say they're going to notice something different about him, and not to say anything about it."

"Oh—so you don't say, 'my big brother is a queer, so get used to it?'"

"Ha haaaaaaa!!!" laughed Rico. "Noooooo!"

I interrupted, "What do you mean, '*notice something different about me*?'"

"It's nothing you notice until you start talking," said Rico.

"Oh, so you think I *talk* gay?" I replied mockingly.

"No, not gay, exactly," said Rico, "just not the way most guys talk."

"Oh," I said in my best rapper imitation, "you mean not like some badass from the 'hood?"

I was glad Bill asked these questions. At least Rico didn't say I *walked gay*. A friend had told me this when I was a teenager—and said that I needed to stop walking *like that*. He'd gone so far as to give me walking lessons, so I could walk more like a straight guy.

I still doubt that actually worked.

Chapter 20

Year Three: Touch

In general, I avoided touching Rico. Even as he grew older and wanted to hug me, or when he put his arm around me or touched my leg when we were at a wrestling meet, I never reciprocated. During his junior and senior years, he tried to hug me fairly often; I instinctively pushed him away. I justified keeping my distance with the rationale that this kept him from being too dependent on me. Eventually he confronted me: "How come you always push me away?"

There was no valid answer. Why should I have denied him a child's right to be hugged? Why was I like this? I still felt somehow... broken, flawed, imperfect.

My parents, especially my mother, tried to hide their disapproval of my sexual orientation, but it surged to the forefront after my initial outing. Throughout my senior year, she put random Bible quotes in my schoolbooks. Anytime the newspaper ran an article about some guy accused of molesting a boy, she would cut it out and slip it under my pillow, or stuff it in my underwear drawer for me to find. There were notes among my things the day I moved out. For years, she continued to send me news clippings of alleged and convicted child molesters.

I read them at first, but they made me feel ashamed. Why did she do this to me? It hurt, but over time I felt sorry for her. It was hard not to be upset when my own mother left me notes indicating that my only possible outcome was to become a pedophile. Eventually, I stopped reading them, and steeled myself against whatever insults people might drum up out of the Bible.

During my teen years, I'd spent weeks and weeks of summer days reading the Bible on the sandy banks of a small island in the ice-cold McKenzie River. I'd pack my Bible and my lunch, and lay in the sun, reading thin page after thin page, trying to understand how God could hate me so much.

I became extremely uncomfortable with displays of affection. I couldn't imagine touching anyone, male or female, in front of my mother. As I grew older, and visited bigger cities, I became especially nervous at the sight of gay people holding hands in public. I felt scared for my life. I felt that if I had done that in Springfield, I'd have been shot dead on the street.

During a visit to my parents' house, in September 2009, all those years of judgmental newspaper clippings roared back to the forefront of my memory. Rico had started wrestling again. He spent quite a bit of time lifting weights and running. During that September visit, Mom and Dad sat with us in the living room while Rico watched TV. He plopped himself face-down on the floor and said, "My legs are really sore. Could you massage them for me?"

My family was not touchy-feely. When it did occur, physical affection was always awkward. As soon as Rico made this request, my mother gave me a strange look.

Well, damned if you do and damned if you don't! If I don't rub his legs, then my parents are going to wonder if this happens all the time, and if I'm not massaging his legs because they're watching! If I do rub his legs, they are going to wonder whether I do this all the time! I can tell by Mom's expression she thinks this is really weird.

In most families, this might not be a big deal, if he were my son, or nephew—or if I were straight.

I struggled in that instant. *Who was I to Rico? Was I a father? A brother? A friend?* This was a Big Brother's four-alarm mental breakdown. I wanted to rebel against this self-censorship. It felt so unfair. *If I were a straight man, would I be this paranoid about what people thought?*

Though it was 30 years since high school, and we lived in less conservative times, in regard to public displays of affection, it was difficult to imagine rubbing a teenage boy's legs without it seeming inappropriate—especially in the same living room where I had declared to my family that I was gay.

Perhaps my 20 years of working around lawyers had taught me a risk-averse life strategy. I'd heard a story about a street-savvy girl who made claims of sexual harassment against her Big Sister —who happened to be a lesbian.

My mind flashed to an imaginary courtroom setting, with my mother seated on the witness stand:

"And what was it that you saw happen on the floor of your living room that night?" asks the lawyer.

"Rico asked my son to rub his legs!" Exclaims my mother.

"Uh-huh—and did that seem at all unusual to you?"

"Oh yes," she'd say. "I thought it was very strange that Rico asked my son to rub his legs! I was even more surprised that my son rubbed them—right in front of me!"

My thoughts returned to Rico, face down on the carpet in front of me, his arms folded and his chin resting on his forearms.

I had to stop thinking. This really wasn't about me, was it?

Rico turned around, as if to ask what was taking me so long. I put my hands on his legs and briefly massaged them. A few seconds later I announced, "There! All done!"

Rico's request was simply his way of showing he was comfortable with me—that, to him, we were all family. How could he know my haunted memories of finding newspaper clippings and Bible quotes in my underwear?

The day after the leg massage incident, Dad lectured Rico, at length, about life in the military: "I was in the Army, but the Navy will be the same way. The main difference is that you'll be out at sea."

It was nice to see my dad start to bond with Rico. As a self-made man, Dad had empathy for Rico's life story. Rico would have to follow the same path to success. And, of course, he had the perfect advice on how Rico should accomplish that.

"The generals and higher-ups will try to get you riled up and to get a reaction out of you," he said. "Just keep your mouth shut and you'll be okay."

That same afternoon, while Rico watched TV in my old bedroom, under the watchful gaze of the deer head, his cell phone buzzed and rang. He gestured, spoke rapidly, and then hung up. His phone rang again. He didn't notice me as I watched from about 30 yards away. His phone calls alternated between two people. He yelled at one of them, hung up, answered another call, spoke briefly and hung up again. I heard him say 'I don't know!' 'I can't talk right now,' and 'I don't want to talk about it!' After several similar conversations, the calls stopped.

David and I were curious to find out what was really going on. We decided to take Rico with us to the gym. As David drove, Rico sat in the back seat with his earbuds plugged in. We could hear the music pounding. David shouted: "So what was going on back there, exactly?"

"What?" asked Rico, as he pulled out an earbud.

"Those phone calls. What were they about?" asked David.

"Oh, nothing," said Rico, as he stuck his earbud back in. "Just my mom."

"That didn't sound like your mother," said David. "It sounded like a girl—a girlfriend?"

Rico was silent.

David continued his questioning; I adjusted the rearview mirror to watch Rico's face. "There was a girl calling you," he said. "You were really rude to her." Suddenly, David's eyes widened. He blurted out, "You got her pregnant!"

Rico pulled out his earbuds, covered his head with his hands and exclaimed, "Wow! You're good!"

"Aha!" said David. "Just what I thought! You got some girl pregnant and she was telling you about it."

Although David has worked mostly with adults, his 25 years as a psychiatrist has given him plenty of insight into the human mind.

Rico immediately confessed, and shared details about the situation. His earlier phone calls alternated between a 14-year-old girl, who had been standing outside his apartment, and his mother. The girl had knocked on the door and told Rico's mother she needed money. Since Rico's mother couldn't understand much English, she was puzzled that Rico owed her money. She didn't recognize the girl, so she kept pressing the redial button on her phone to ask him what it was the girl wanted. Simultaneously, the girl called Rico and demanded he ask his mother to give her some cash for a pregnancy test kit.

"Were you using a condom?" David demanded.

"Yeah, but it broke," said Rico. "I haven't seen her in a couple of weeks, anyway."

Rico asked several questions about the likelihood of condoms breaking during sex, and whether the withdrawal method was effective in preventing pregnancy.

"Not really," I said. "So… do you think you're the father?"

Rico was dismissive. "I just want her to have an abortion! I never want to talk to her again!"

I could see that he was reacting out of fear.

"I only told my best friends about having sex with that girl," he said, "but she's telling a lot of her friends and people are talking about it at school." Then he defended himself: "A lot of boys have slept with her—not just me!"

So he slept with her because she was easy? Oh, great.

"That doesn't matter. They can do a paternity test to find out who the father is… and that father will owe child support for 18 years." I wanted to make myself very clear. "It doesn't matter how many guys slept with her, what matters is what sperm fertilized the egg and created the baby." By this point, I felt exasperated and worried that this was going to end badly. I didn't like feeling as if I were channeling my father.

When we got to the gym, David and I conferred, and told Rico we thought he should have the girl contact Planned Parenthood for an appointment, rather than buying her a pregnancy test kit. He took our advice. The next day he said he hadn't heard anything else from her.

I called our match support specialist. "He's disclosed being sexually active," said Ellen. "You should talk to him about whatever you feel comfortable with." She followed up with an email containing links to websites about teen relationships, STDs and pregnancy.

I reminded myself about our Friendship Agreement—and the rules against keeping secrets. My agreement with Big Brothers/Big Sisters required me to report such incidents. I left a voicemail about the situation with his state caseworker, Cindy. A week went by without a call back from her.

This was an extremely difficult position for me. If I had been an uncle, or a neighbor—just a friend, or any relative, really—I would only need to counsel Rico on his best course of action. But if I did that, it would be considered keeping a secret from his mother—and from the system that tried to protect him. I didn't want to do that, either. I had written obligations. Could our relationship ever recover if he considered me a snitch? I wondered if he would ever reveal anything of importance again, or hide even more things from me. At his age, that's what I would have done.

And that's exactly what he did, too.

Photo courtesy: Timothy Oakley

Chapter 21

Year Four:
Fall 2009 (10th Grade)

The following week Rico had a summer mud run at Trask Mountain. It was an informal annual event attended by all area high schools with cross-country teams. David and I drove for over an hour to the event to show our support. We videotaped him, and captured a few photos as well.

From the second he knew I was there, Rico refused to acknowledge me. His anger distressed me. I confronted him. "You KNOW that I'm your Big Brother. I'm not allowed to keep stuff like that secret."

He still ignored me. I went home that day feeling depressed. Rico must have felt the same sense of betrayal that I had experienced, 30 years earlier, with my parents. In the end, nothing I said to his caseworker about the paternity scare was of any help for Rico: before long, she just gave up on him. I was still upset over the situation. Once again, David reminded me that I'd fulfilled my written obligation to Rico.

"You've had four years together. Those four years were good. But maybe now's a good time to start over."

If I quit Rico, it would feel like I'd failed him. He still showed a lot of promise, and I understood exactly why he was upset with me. Worried that I had ruined the trust it took me four years for me to earn, I wrote my first truly heartfelt letter to Rico, trying to explain myself.

Letter Part I

September 25, 2009

Dear Rico:

I am writing this letter to you for several reasons. A couple of things have happened in your life recently that concern me. Mostly, they have served to make me feel that I have failed you. Not necessarily because of what you did, but because I can't tell if they are things that you are sorry about.

Dealing with these issues is excruciatingly difficult for me. Not only because I am having to face the fact that you are growing up (and that means I am getting older too!) but because it brings back to me so many good and bad memories of my own childhood and my teenage friends.

One of the things I know about you is that on the inside you are a total marshmallow. You don't like to show it, but I know it is there. You are a very kind and caring person. It is distressing to me to know that you had to endure so many difficult experiences at a young age. When I first met you it was clear that you did not particularly trust adults. Although you have never spoken to me much about your early childhood, you did tell me about some incidents that left me with the impression that perhaps you suffered some severe emotional traumas. These might be things that to an adult might not seem serious, but they were serious to you. And because they were serious to you, they were important. I am so sorry that whatever those things were, I was not there to help you.

After we first met, I was a little concerned by the fact that it took you well over a year to really start talking to me. You were pretty clammed up. You never told me about your court hearings or your lawyer, your therapist/counselor, or your worries or fears. The closest thing you ever came to revealing any fear to me was when you asked, "Will you be my big brother forever?" I was a little afraid that maybe you wanted to exchange me for someone else. Like I should have some kind of expiration date. I told you that I would be your big brother as long as you want me.

In the last 25 years I have hardly cried at all about anything. I cried in 1986 when one of my boyfriends found out he had AIDS. I cried in 1990 over a lover who killed himself because he was HIV-positive. I cried so much at my friend Russell's drug and alcohol intervention in '97 that I could barely talk. I cried in 2000 when I met David, and then at our wedding in 2003.

And then, in 2006, on my third visit to see you, after I dropped you off, I sat in the car and I cried really, really hard. It was that day I realized how lucky I was to have you in my life. Not just because I could do things for you, but because you do so much for me. You have taught me so many things and enriched my life in so many ways that I cannot thank you enough. I will never be able to express how much you mean to me. I only hope that as you grow older you will come to think of me as a true brother and as someone who will be there for you always.

As time passes, you will learn which people are your real friends and which ones are not. Generally, real friends don't give you advice unless you ask for it. This is why it is so hard for me to give you advice without you asking me. I figure you have enough people telling you what to do. It is my preference to bring knowledge and enlightenment to your life through demonstration rather than lecturing.

…You've met my father. He never met a lecture he didn't like. He doesn't lecture nearly as much as he did 35 years ago, but he still tells some of the same stories. And the same jokes. When I was your age I couldn't stand my father. Now I consider him among my dearest friends. And I am starting to face up to how much I will miss him one day when he is gone. If you had told me that when I was 15 I would have said you were completely insane. But that is the kind of thing that changes as you get older; people change, and relationships change. My dad barely hid his anger and was very controlling. You know why he almost never had to spank me? Because I was terrified of him when he was mad.

So now I feel as if in some ways I am in my father's shoes. I am coming to face the fact that you are growing up. You're old enough now that your body has provided you with the capacity to create human life. And part of you growing up means that I need to start talking to you like an adult. That is still difficult for me in person. I was raised in a family where there were a lot of things that we just never discussed. And so I wrote. It is why I am writing to you now. You should know that I have taken very seriously every word that I am writing to you here.

Letter – Part II

The Lecture

First off, regarding the shoplifting, you were very lucky that the store did not decide to prosecute you. What bothered me even more than the fact that you took something, aside from the fact that you seem to have always gotten practically everything you always want, is that rather than being sorry for what you had done, you sat in the security office counting the number of cameras they had. That is troublesome to me because it speaks to your state of mind at the time.

Secondly, regarding the sexual episode, you did not voluntarily share that information with me. I did not tell your caseworker that you got a girl pregnant exactly. But I didn't feel like arguing with you. Aside from that, the information David and I got out of you was only by questioning you, practically as an interrogation. It brings me no pleasure. But that was another serious incident. Again, it was not so much the fact that you had sex but the fact that you wanted to kick a potentially pregnant 14 year old girl to the curb. That does not speak highly of you.

It is important for you to remember that if you are having sex with someone, you must accept responsibility for the potential consequence of becoming a father, or contracting any one of a number of sexually transmitted diseases, including some that are life-threatening. Last year, there were 9.4 million cases of STDs diagnosed for young people ages 15-24 in the U.S. Up to 40% of all teenage girls in the US have some kind of STD.

You have seen the abortion pictures at OMSI. Clearly you know what an abortion actually is. It is not good for you to have a callous disregard for another human life just because it is not your own. I know you better than that and while it was probably fear motivating you to say those things, it is important to remember that your actions speak loudly and your words also have an impact on yourself and others - far greater than you can imagine.

You probably think of me as a very liberal person. In many ways I am. However, I am not generally in favor of abortions. I also believe in a woman's right to choose. It is not my body and I think women should have the right to choose, whether they agree with me or not. Put yourself in her position. No girl you ever get pregnant will let you make that decision for her.

If a girl is pregnant and decides to have the baby, you will be responsible for paying child support until the child is 18 years old. No matter where you live, the government will hunt you down and take the money out of your paycheck every single month. If you can't pay, they will let a debt pile up on account and it will accrue interest until it is an enormous debt that you cannot recover from. It can wreck your life, and I have seen it happen.

Rico, just think about your own life. Wouldn't you have rather had a father? If you get a girl pregnant and she keeps the baby, which happens most of the time, are you really going to want to have nothing to do with your own child?

Would you inflict on another human being the kind of suffering you have endured yourself as a result of your own father's behavior? Would you really? I think I know you well enough to say that I don't think you could honestly want that for any child, least of all your own.

For both of these incidents, because I am participating in the Big Brother/Big Sister program, it is not up to me to not report what is happening in your life. That is why I want you to be a good student and focus on what matters most in your life right now—studying, being involved in things at school, and preparing yourself for your future career, whatever you decide you want that to be. I am not an asshole, and I don't like playing one in your life.

With love from your Big Brother,

–Aaron

I didn't mention my desperate moments of wanting to give up. Some things weren't right to reveal to him. There were limits to displaying weakness to a teenager!

Rico got my letter, but he never said anything about it. A week later, he called to ask if we could do something together. When we did meet, he said he hadn't been to see a dentist in over a year. As I dropped him off that night, his mother complained he hadn't been doing his chores. I asked Rico to help out around the house, like he was supposed to.

The next day I talked to his caseworker, and learned that Rico had dental insurance and she would get something done about that. The next time I saw him, a couple weeks later, he had gone to the dentist and spent a lot of time cleaning up the apartment.

A letter arrived from Russell:

Dear Aaron:

I'm writing in response to your letter. It's great to hear from you—not so great to hear of all the challenges in your life with family. Thank God you're in a position to be a solid support. It's got to be frustrating with Rico. I know my parents went through hell. With all the opportunity and privileges my life still somehow seemed destined to follow the path it has.

I've been walking the track at night with a friend who has no regrets because his path has led to his current relationship with God. As for me, it's everything I can do to keep my sight off of the many mistakes along the way. I remember my dad asking me one time if I thought counseling or a trip to a ranch might be helpful. Of course at 15 I denied needing any help. Oh how blind, scared, and full of pride I've been. The trip to a ranch was something that a friend of mine did as a youth and I hear he's in a California prison now. So I guess sometimes all we can do is keep loving the best we can. I know that's not much help.

The whole parenting thing is a trip. I know I've been terrible at it. I guess it's that knowledge that helps me have that much more respect for our parents. I know there were times I wish dad was more a friend, but to what end? I somehow think that by 15 our future is pretty well mapped out—we are, for all intents and purposes adults by then. Maybe that's why my kids are doing ok—'cause I am out of the way? I really don't know. The older I get, the less I really know.

Love, Russell

It wasn't right to give up on Rico just yet. David and I were planning a trip to Germany. We decided to use it as a motivator. David's niece was engaged to an Indianapolis Wal-Mart executive whose maternal family was from Germany. During our vacation, we'd have several days to visit other cities. We told Rico that if he studied harder, and got As and Bs like he had done in junior high, we would take him with us.

At Rico's next court hearing, the judge supported this idea, and encouraged Rico to try harder at school so he could take advantage of this travel opportunity.

Chapter 22

Therapy

Despite the guidance of my match specialist—and a psychiatrist on call in my own home—I still needed direction on how to approach what felt like a raft of crises.

I needed to talk to someone about all the roles in my life these days: Big Brother, parent and son. I could change hats more fluidly now, but it still felt complicated. Chief among the issues that confronted me was the fact that Rico needed to pull up his grades (and pants!) and needed to focus on graduation. If he didn't get through high school on time, he could say goodbye to plans for joining the Navy. He would have to go to college or get a low-wage job.

I needed a neutral third-party. I needed a therapist.

Linda was a plump, pleasant-looking 60-something woman with a comfortable office in Northwest Portland. Each time we met, I relaxed in a cushy leather armchair as she sat, facing me, in her rocking chair. The room was filled with natural light, and had rows of books, a floor lamp, a roll top desk and a large Persian rug.

Linda was soft spoken and nodded her head a lot. As we spoke, she drew circles on her pad and dashed words along radiating lines. It was nice to have someone actively listen. Linda never gave a quick solution; she took time to reflect and to ask questions.

"So—you wanted to talk about Rico?"

"That's right..." it felt embarrassing to seek psychological help. Though Rico was my primary reason for counseling, there were other issues with my parents and at work. I had been at a new law firm for four months. The company seemed on the verge of bankruptcy. So far, no paychecks had bounced—and my current benefits included several free counseling sessions with Linda.

The professional staff of Big Brothers/Big Sisters was incredibly supportive, but something more was needed. It sometimes felt as if my match specialist were giving me cotton candy when I really needed a steak—and that's saying a lot for a vegetarian. I needed to be more able to process things, and to prepare for whatever the future with Rico might bring.

It didn't seem fair to ask a match support person for such in-depth assistance. They could barely keep up with safety checks on hundreds of other matches. And while there were dozens of books about mentoring college graduates in the workplace, there didn't seem to be any on being a life coach to an at-risk youth. I needed my own life coach.

As I relaxed into the room around me, I tried to be in the present moment. I exhaled deeply, leaned back in the chair and folded my hands behind my head.

"He was just caught shoplifting. And then he had a close call with getting a 14-year-old girl pregnant."

"Oh," she said in a serious tone, as she drew loopy circles on her doodle pad. "Well, yes, that is a concern," she nodded. I wondered if she were drawing a Venn diagram of my life.

"I'm not judging him. I shoplifted from a store once and practically everyone I know did the same thing as a teenager. What bothered me about his shoplifting was the fact that once the police came, and he was escorted to the security office, instead of being nervous and feeling bad about his actions, he counted the number of security cameras and tried to figure out their locations by looking at the TV monitors!"

"Well," she said, "you can ask him questions that force him to see where his choices will lead, and then whatever conclusion he reaches—you can ask whether that's what he really wants. If he makes a bad choice, you can also reverse the process by asking him what choices he made that led to this particular outcome. Don't try to make him get everything right. We all have to make mistakes."

I started using her advice. And, when challenging situations arose, I saved my questions to ask her later.

At our next visit I explained, "Rico told me he didn't want to do his homework because he's mad at his mom and thinks it's a good way to get back at her."

"Get back at her for what?" she asked.

I shrugged. *Who knew?*

She nodded and doodled. Her doodling had a hypnotic, calming magic. She repeating her advice from the previous week—I must have needed to hear it again.

"Sometimes," she said, "we have to let children fail. If they tell us they are going to do something that we know is going to have a bad outcome, the best thing we can do is to try to get them to see forward into the future, and think about the consequences their actions can have."

"For example," she said, "if he says he's going to skip class or not do his homework because that's a way for him to get back at his mother because, as you say, he's angry with her—something you might do is ask him, 'And how do you think that will work out for you?'"

In hindsight, my biggest failure as a Big Brother was my belief that, because Rico started at some supposed disadvantage in life, I could be Superman and make everything perfect. Over time, it became clear that wasn't possible. There were many potential drivers behind his behavior, once he went to live with his mother: failure, self-doubt, emotional loss and bitterness—perhaps even revenge.

"Don't be too hard on yourself," Linda said, looking up from her doodle pad. "What he needs, more than anything, is for you to be a friend. He has all kinds of people judging him. His mother, his teachers, his peers, the DHS caseworkers, his family therapist… what he really needs from you is someone to be there and to listen. Be consistent in your own behavior and just be someone who cares."

It was good advice—I seemed to hear it from everyone. It made me begin to wonder if Rico didn't need a father, a brother or a friend. Maybe he needed someone who stuck around.

My last major topic with Linda was my parents. Their lives were overwhelmed by the stress of aging. Dad had gone completely blind. He had lost his balance and was at constant risk of falling. A few times he had hit his head on the brick fireplace and the coffee table. My mother's rheumatoid arthritis made it difficult for her to take care of him by herself. Dad would soon need in-home care.

He could still dress himself if Mom put out a pile of clothes. He couldn't cook, but could feed himself when food was put in front of him. About the only time Dad got a shower was when I forced him to take one, every few weeks when I visited.

My father's slow physical decline led him to become severely depressed. He talked about his childhood and obsessed over the sudden realization that, as a boy, my grandpa had contracted him out as a day laborer and kept all his wages to buy beer and cigarettes.

After we'd built up weeks of rapport, it seemed appropriate to share with Linda another issue that had really been bothering me. "One day after Mom left the house to take her Chihuahua to the groomers, Dad put a gun to his head and tried to kill himself. He didn't know that my sister had taken all his bullets. When Mom got home she found him sitting in the bedroom next to his hand-scrawled note. It said she would be better off without him. On our next visit, David yelled at him for not thinking about what a horrible thing it would have been for my mom to come home and find him dead in their bedroom. He calmed down after that but blamed my brother for taking his bullets and messing everything up."

"It's important to know," Linda responded, "that as our parents age they are in a time of transition. It's possible they have a lot of things they've been carrying around for years that they might want to share."

And a few weeks later, they did.

Chapter 23

Home on the Range

As my employer-sponsored therapy sessions ended, I tried to appreciate being fully alive.

Later that week, another letter came from Russell. Its subject was old age, which seemed timely.

> Dear Aaron:
>
> Hi brother! Hadn't heard from you in a while so wanted to touch base. Last letter I got seemed somewhat bleak, between hauling your dad around and begging God to instill some insight into Rico. How is Rico?
>
> Part of me wants to move on to the great beyond before I have to experience the full brunt of old age. Lord knows I don't deserve such mercy, but I'm really counting on grace to carry me through. You know I've met all kinds of people from all kinds of backgrounds and what I'm coming to realize is that we're going to do what we're gonna do and no amount of persuasion from people, loved or not, wisdom from God or opportunity in life seems to be able to change a path that has seemingly been already laid out since before our awareness. So I guess what we gotta do is just keep loving through it all because that's about the only healthy thing we can do for ourselves and for each other.

I actually envy your life of crisis because it means you're doing some real living and not hiding behind one of so many masks we can wear. If you want, encourage Rico to write me. At the very least I can offer some sort of commonality that might help him make more informed choices. I know it really will take an act of God. Hell, I've gotten one letter from my kids in the last year. I've lived such a selfish and indulgent life I'm amazed to have the family I do, including you.

God bless you and your family—all of them. Take care.

Love, Russell.

A few days later, David and I took a trip to Springfield to visit Mom for her birthday. As soon as we arrived, Dad began to protest his attending a four-week out-of- state VA training program for the blind. He didn't want to go because it was farther from my mother than he had been in over 50 years. "I'll go if my doctor says it's OK," said Dad.

David replied: "I am one of your doctors, Bob, and it's OK!"

"But I might have a heart attack!" Dad protested, lying nearly flat in his forest green La-Z-Boy.

"Bob," David replied, "you'll be staying in a hospital! Having angina pains at a hospital is the best place you can be!"

The next day, Mom sat on the floral-patterned couch under the gold cherubs as Dad and I reclined in the matching forest green La-Z-Boys. An episode of *CSI* blared from the TV. Patches the Chihuahua was curled up on a 20-year-old handmade lime green afghan.

I looked around the room at the aging white carpet, dotted with spots where the dog had peed on it. It was cleaned periodically, but though they could afford to replace it, Mom and Dad didn't want the inconvenience.

Suddenly, Dad shut off his books-on-tape machine and pulled off his headphones. As he stared straight ahead, he loudly exclaimed: "When you were born, your mother didn't even want to look at you!"

"What?" I asked.

My mother frowned at him.

"Zip it, Bob!"

He chuckled, scratched his head, and went on. "After you were born, your mother heard you were a boy and had the nurses take you away. She didn't want to see you for a long time. *She wanted a girl*!"

My mouth dropped open.

Dad kept talking. "Both your brother and sister were born bald-headed! But you had a thick head of jet black hair. I wondered if you even belonged to me!" And then, in reference to the fact that in those days we had milk delivered to the front door, he added, "I thought you must have belonged to the milkman!"

Neither of us said anything. He shrugged, put his headphones back on, and pressed PLAY on his books-on-tape machine.

David and I left after breakfast the next morning. A few days later I received a letter from Mom:

Dear Aaron:

Why your dad today out of the blue mentioned how I felt when you were born is beyond me. I got over my feelings (immature) and hope you know that.

Sometimes Bob's remarks about people really get to me, but to no *avail* if I point this out to him. So he still does this awful habit.

I apologize and hope you understand.

Hope your day went ok otherwise.

Love, Mom.

Chapter 24

Year Four
(10ᵗʰ Grade)

One day, Rico decided to share something with me about himself.

"I'm a sensitive guy to most people and hard to a few," he said.

"Who are you hard to?"

"Girls."

"Why is that?"

"Because," he smirked, "girls will run off and cry and then come back wanting attention even more. Then they want to know what is wrong with them."

This sounded exactly like something one of my straight guy friends would say. If I had ever had any doubt that Rico was heterosexual, it would have vanished after hearing a statement like that.

Ahh—the life of a straight teen! It was so different than things had been for me.

Chapter 25

Rewind: 1977

At 16, I regularly sneaked out of the house at night to meet up with my boyfriend Mark. Our highly choreographed plan, in the pre-cell phone era, would impress any wayward teen of today. It involved arriving at a designated spot at an agreed-upon time. If either of us didn't show up within five minutes of the rendezvous time, we tried again the following night.

My routine was to escape—either through my bedroom window or through the garage. Crawling out the window wasn't easy, and carried a special set of risks—like the neighbor's barking dog. My window's aluminum frames were very sharp, and any stumble to the ground could result in the unwanted clanging of any of a number of 1930s hobo knickknacks Mom had decorating the patio.

We also had a snoopy neighbor lady who would stick her head out her back door, at the slightest commotion, to see what was going on. It was better to sneak out the door through the garage, which was directly adjacent to my room.

On the nights I took the garage route, my heart rate increased significantly. I had to pull my bedroom door shut behind me in the dark and turn the doorknob that would lead me into the garage. I couldn't turn on any lights since there was no way to turn them off before I used the side door to the backyard.

If my mother came out to do a load of laundry, or grab something from the garage pantry, it would foil my escape. Although it never happened, I imagined myself trying to freeze in some Monty-Python-esque tableau, hoping to become invisible standing in the middle of the room.

One night, as I left my room and opened the door to the darkened garage, I stood in the silence, sniffing. The air seemed pungent, yet strangely refreshing. My eyes adjusted to the darkness with the help of a faint streetlight that shined in a far window. The light struck an object somewhere across the room. It appeared at least five or six feet away from me. I took two steps towards it—and slammed face first into the cold damp flesh of a freshly skinned deer.

I ran outside, stifling a scream.

That summer was filled with days of visiting Mark at his house after work. When I went to his house, I always made sure to park several blocks away. One day my dad figured out the neighborhood where Mark lived. We huddled inside the kitchen house and listened to Dad's barely muffled Chevy pickup roar up and down the street. He finally drove away, unable to figure out my location. When I got home later that day, Dad told me it was a good thing he couldn't find us, because he was packing heat.

That was such typical Springfield behavior! When something pissed you off, you just shot it.

Chapter 26

Year Four: December 2009

One day, as I picked up Rico at his apartment, his mother Maria pointed out a big hole Rico had punched in the wall. They had it hidden behind a calendar. Seeing the fist-sized hole made me glad Rico didn't have access to guns—as far as I knew.

Maria told me she thought Rico needed anger management counseling. There was an apartment inspection coming up and Maria was worried they might be thrown out if the landlord saw the hole in the sheetrock. Fortunately, she found someone to repair it.

Rico had talked a lot about being angry lately. Late one night after a movie, as we drove to his home, his mother called him on his cellphone.

"I told you I was going to a movie!" he said in English. She rapidly replied in Spanish. He replied as quickly and forcefully back to her in Spanish. By the time he hung up, we were just a couple of miles from his house.

"What was that about?"

"I told her three times today that I was going to be with you tonight and she keeps acting like I didn't tell her. She is so stupid!" It wasn't the first time Rico called his mother stupid.

Rico asked me how you could tell someone was gay. "You can't always tell," I replied. He asked me over and over—and I offered the same answer.

"Why aren't you answering my question?"

"Why do you want to know?"

"There's a guy at my school I think is gay and I want to beat him up," he said.

"Just beating someone up is not such a great idea; you'll just get suspended or expelled. How would you like it if someone beat you up for being Latino?"

He didn't answer. "Why did you slam your fist into the wall at your apartment?"

"Someone moved my video game controller," he said.

"Look, it's normal to get angry about things sometimes, but not over little things like that. You need to learn how to control your anger, and not let it control you. Something like that could get your family kicked out of your apartment. Where would you go? When I was your age, I would get really angry at my parents. What I did, when I couldn't hold it inside anymore, was to take a glass jar out into the backyard and smash it onto the pavement as hard as possible. I know it sounds weird, but it always made me feel better."

Like a true neat freak, I added, "Just don't leave a mess. Clean it up and throw the glass in the trash so your little brother doesn't step in it." I don't know if he ever took my suggestion.

Rico's anger seemed to abate when wrestling practice started up again. His mother and sister stopped complaining about his behavior. It appeared that physical exercise helped keep his darker impulses at bay.

Complaints about his anger made me wonder if, like Russell, he was involved in some troublemaking he didn't talk about.

I hoped he would always tell me the truth, no matter how difficult it was for him. To experiment, I confessed a lie. Our conversations sometimes felt strained, and I didn't like it. We needed to keep building a bridge between us. In the car one day, I said:

"We shouldn't have secrets from each other. It's important that we be honest. There's something I lied to you about a few years ago. I think now you're old enough for me to tell you the truth. Do you remember when you were 12 and you asked me if I ever smoked pot? I said I never had, remember? Well, that was a lie. I did smoke pot," adding quickly, "—but not until I was 18!"

I followed up my confession with a five-minute lecture. "Marijuana is especially bad for anyone under 22 because the human brain is still growing and it can literally make you stupid... Aside from that, it makes it virtually impossible to focus on schoolwork, or just about anything else."

I assumed would respond by telling me he had smoked pot more than the one time he'd already admitted.

Rico paused and looked down. He was clearly thinking about something. Then he turned to me and said, "My mom told me the truth about my dad."

"What?"

"She was raped by her sister's husband."

"Wait—what?"

"My aunt isn't married to him anymore. No one knows where he is," he said. "He's in southern California somewhere. I used to want to meet my dad. Not anymore."

I was dumbfounded.

What would it have felt like to find out, as a 15-year-old boy, that my mother had been raped by my father? My heart ached for him.

If Rico was devastated by the news, he hid it well. It was clear he had been thinking about it for a long time. His anger toward his mother—and the world at large—suddenly made a lot more sense.

I could see why he called his mother names. It wasn't really logical, since she was the victim, but it was clear he felt betrayed and hurt in ways I couldn't understand. He had been acting out his frustration. Maria damaged his self-image, and he had been internalizing it for weeks. I wished he had told me sooner.

Chapter 27

Year Four: February 2010 (10th Grade)

One Saturday morning in February, I went to Rico's apartment to pick him up. After parking, I sent him a text message to come outside. Several minutes passed and he didn't show up, so I got out to go knock at the door.

As I reached the front porch, Rico opened the door, visibly upset. He faced inside and yelled in Spanish. His mother shouted back. Rico lashed out in one final angry barrage and then turned toward me. He slammed the front door behind him. He passed me as he headed across the lawn toward the car. He stumbled a little. Tears were running down his cheeks.

As he got in the car, he continued to look down and wipe his eyes. He'd never cried so openly before in my presence. I sat in the driver's seat and waited quietly as he looked out the window away from me into the rain.

"What's wrong?" I asked. He was silent. "Look, that's why I'm here—you can tell me anything."

I took a deep breath.

He wiped his eyes again. "She was yelling at me to pull up my pants!" he said. "She said that I shouldn't let my pants hang down in front of you because you're gay and that is tempting you. She is always saying stuff like that."

Her comments struck me as so ridiculous that I laughed out loud. I wished she would fight that hard with him to go to school!

"Look," I said, "compared to all the other things I've heard in my life, that one is actually pretty funny. It's an interesting theory." I didn't like his saggy pants any more than his mother, and often made fun of them myself. But her comments were hurtful. As Rico wiped tears from his face, I asked, "What were you yelling back at her?"

"I told her you've done more for me than she ever has."

"That's really nice of you to say, Rico. I appreciate you defending me. But you know your mom has done a lot for you. She works hard to keep a roof over your head and food on the table. So while she is working you and me can go out and have fun."

Everyone made it harder for me to handle Rico—including his mother. I could understand if her underlying motivation was to get him to pull his pants up. Saying bad things about me was not going to get her what she wanted. If anything, Rico would wear them slung even lower, to piss us off even more.

Since he had been hanging out with me almost every week for four years, it seemed that Rico's perception of gay men couldn't be all that negative.

I was surprised to find out how wrong that assumption would be.

While doing homework a couple weeks later, Rico mentioned, in an offhand manner, that he had written some answers to questions for social studies that he wanted me to read.

"Sure," I said, as he looked through his backpack.

"Oh," he said. He looked at me and stuffed his papers back inside as he zipped the bag back up. "I guess I left the questions at home."

"Can't you read me your answers?"

"No, it's not the same. You need to hear the questions."

He had barely looked through his papers before he stuffed them back into his bag. Rico almost never talked to me about homework. This must have been something he really did want to talk about. I was suspicious. Maybe he lost his nerve?

I brought it up again in the car on the way home later that night.

"So what was that assignment about again?"

"Oh. It was about the court case in Florida. About those lesbian mothers who are trying to adopt. We had to write a paper arguing if we thought it was right or wrong."

"And you said…"

"I don't think they should be able to," said Rico.

"They who?"

"Gays and lesbians," he said.

"Why not?"

"There is just no replacement for a mother's love," he said. "You gotta agree with me there."

He was so wrong. First off, he was the one who always called his mother stupid. My mother and I had well-known disagreements. Now Rico was telling me there was nothing equal to that dysfunction?

"So wait. I'm confused. Are you saying that a baby being put up for adoption can't be adopted by two lesbians? Even if their birth mother doesn't want them? You think it would be better for them to be orphans?"

"If they want to have a baby, they can get a sperm donor."

"But you don't think they would make good parents?" David was a sperm donor for a lesbian couple who had a baby. Rico had met them, and David's daughter. I wondered if because he knew lesbians who had a sperm donor, he made any kind of exception to his rule about gay parenting.

Rico tried to interrupt me; feeling indignant and defensive, I pressed on. "You don't think I'd make a good dad?" My question took him by surprise. He stopped talking. I couldn't tell if he was thinking about it, or if he felt he didn't want to make me mad and was keeping his mouth shut.

A few minutes later we said our goodbyes. As I drove away, I hoped he felt a little guilty about what he'd said to me.

Rico remained silent on gay issues for a few weeks. Then he said, somewhat arrogantly, "If they come out of the closet we disown them, but they can get married and have children and carry on secretly."

I couldn't figure out who the "we" who disowned gay people were. Had he heard this from some of his extended family members? It felt like he was taunting me, trying out these opinions to see if what he said out loud was something he really felt, and to see if I objected.

As Rico got a heavy dose of MSNBC and democratic politics from David and me—the liberal Reform Jews—he also faced the influences of environmental and cultural pushback.

I cut him some slack. After all, I said things I didn't really believe when I was his age, including: "I have a girlfriend," and "nice tits!" I figured that, in the end, I would be a better example of a man than the deadbeat dads that had fathered him and his siblings.

As the one male consistently present in Rico's life, his mother often complained to me about his backtalk. She asked me if I could try to do something about it. Rico and I talked about the importance of respecting his mother because she worked hard to support him. Still, I was there for Rico, not his mother. If that tactic didn't work, I couldn't fight that battle for her.

One day, in the car, I once again reminded him of his responsibility to do what his mother told him. He turned to me and yelled: "You're not my dad!"

His remark stung, but I knew trying to act as a dad had failed.

"I know I'm not your dad. And you know what? I feel really sorry for him. It's too bad he didn't get a chance to know you because you're a really great guy, Rico. I'm lucky to have you in my life."

He was quiet after that. I wondered whether it was just his way of telling me he didn't want a *gay* dad.

Chapter 28

Year Five: June 2010

One summer afternoon, Rico's leadership qualities really impressed me. He had asked me to pick him up at a park, where he was hanging out with friends. When I got there, Rico was quarterbacking a flag football game. I was surprised he knew how to play football, much less run quarterback. It was impressive to see a 16-year-old call out plays and give orders—and that a half dozen teenage boys let him call the shots.

He was so much like Russell. His leadership abilities gave him power. I hoped he would use his skills in a positive way.

After the game was over, we walked to the car together. I said, "You know, Rico, you have the qualities of a real leader." It impressed me to see him take charge like that. It felt like I had rarely praised him. It seemed important for me to encourage him more often. A lot of teenage boys are followers. They need more positive leaders.

Rico was surprised by the compliment.

"Really?" he asked. "Why do you say that?"

"Because of the way you were shouting orders out there and all those guys were listening to you."

"Aw. That's nothing. Someone has to do it."

We all have qualities we don't see in ourselves—even if we see them in others. Rico could be proud of his leadership abilities. A lot of people wanted (or tried) to lead, but rarely was anyone effective at the job. He could be such a person—if I could figure out a way for him to get leadership training.

Clearly, Rico could take control of his life if he wanted to. At his age, I wasn't left with much choice.

Chapter 29

Rewind:
May 1979

In the spring of my senior year, about three months before I turned 18, my parents let me spend a week visiting an aunt who lived nearby. I'm not sure why, although Dad probably decided to go fishing and Mom wanted a break from her three teenagers. It turned out that my aunt was in the process of divorcing her husband—my mother's youngest brother. As a helpful and practical teenager, I passed along to my aunt a book recommended by a friend. Called *Creative Divorce*, it detailed ways to minimize the typical emotional upheavals of the process. It explained all the various stages involved in separation.

It was an act I would later come to regret.

One day, not long after my return home, I sat at the piano, singing to myself. My mother knocked on my bedroom door. She looked upset. I feared Mom had somehow found out that, during my visit, I got drunk one night on something she called a Sloe Gin Fizz. That wasn't it. Mom was upset about me giving my aunt the book.

"I just got home from Denman's baseball game," she said. "He was crying and talking about that book you gave his wife. I've never seen him cry before. Not in my whole life!"

Her family had obvious issues in displaying human emotions. I shrugged and walked back to the piano. I turned to look at her as she stood in the doorway, across the expanse of freshly raked avocado green shag carpeting. We were separated by one set of footprints, but an ocean of emotion.

In my early school years, my parents put an upright grand piano under the huge gun rack in my bedroom. Mom paid a lot of money for my piano lessons. I rarely practiced, but every now and then a single song really got to me. I would play it over and over again for hours on end. The night she came out to my room, I was playing a popular ABBA song called "Departure".

I sat back down and began the song again. Although she had interrupted me, the words seemed to carry more meaning with every passing second.

It was inevitable that she would interrupt me again. I passive-aggressively invited her to sit next to me by scooting to the left side of the bench.

The song continued, its words echoing my sense of excitement over leaving our sad little town.

Soon, I felt mother hovering at my side. She interrupted, "Why did you do that?"

"Do what?" I asked, still afraid she would ask me about the Sloe Gin Fizz.

"Why did you give her *that book*?"

"I don't know, Mom. I thought I was helping."

She turned around, and closed my bedroom door behind her as she left.

I played and sang on, taking in the song's sense of unknowing what would lie in store for me once I finally moved out. Still, I was hopeful.

How I longed for the day I would turn 18. Soon there was another knock at my door. Mom was back. I opened the door a crack.

"What?"

"I want to come in."

"What for?"

"I want to know why you gave my brother's wife that book."

She was exhausting me. "I told you, Mom. I'm sorry. There's nothing I can do about it now." I closed the door and locked it. I rested my forehead against its imitation walnut hollowness. I heard nothing from the other side, and walked back across the green shag.

There was another knock at the door. By now the carpet looked trampled. It was so irritating—now I'd have to rake it again.

"WHAT!"

"Let me in," she commanded.

"No." I replied calmly.

"Open the door!" she said.

Something inside me snapped. Maybe it was the combination of Bible quotes, the creepy psychiatrist and the pedophile newspaper articles. I'd finally had enough.

"MOM! WILL. YOU. JUST. FUCK. OFF!"

Instantly besieged with guilt, I gasped and covered my mouth. I'd never sworn at my mother before. This had crossed some invisible line, but I didn't care. I was fed up.

Thirty seconds later, Dad pounded his fists on my bedroom door.

"OPEN THIS DOOR! You can't talk to your mother like that!"

"Dad, she is driving me crazy! I told her I'm sorry! There's nothing else I can do."

He refused to listen. "OPEN THIS DOOR RIGHT NOW OR I'M GOING TO BREAK IT DOWN!"

I knew he wasn't kidding. I backed up a few steps and prepared myself as I yelled back, "Well you're gonna have to knock it down because I'm not gonna open it!"

Seconds later—in what felt like slow motion—the door flew toward me. Splinters of wood soared through the air. I fell back onto my waterbed. Before I knew it, he was punching me in the face. The bed sloshed wildly as I struggled under his weight. I managed to slug him in the head, which knocked off his glasses and bloodied his nose. I relished the fact that I was able to fight back with some resistance.

As soon as the fight broke out, my mother ran to the kitchen to phone her brother. Minutes later, one of my mom's other brothers was pushing us apart.

After Uncle Ron took my dad into the next room, I realized I was late for work. As the adults sat in the living room, I gathered some things together and got into my 1967 Buick Special. I drove off, singing through my tears.

Once at work, I called my uncle's house. My aunt Lisa answered. "Can I stay with you?" I asked, "I don't care if I have to sleep in my car, I am not going back there until I am 18!"

"I'll have to talk to your uncle," she said.

A few minutes later she called back. "You can stay here."

I was grateful to know I wouldn't have to sleep in my car.

A couple weeks later, as I was in my room reading, Uncle Ron knocked on the door. "Your mother's on the phone," he said. "She wants to know if she can come see you."

I was hopeful. *Oh, how sweet! She must be overwhelmed with guilt!* I imagined us eating ice cream together at Dairy Queen, where she would apologize for her misunderstanding. Everything would work out fine. Based on my happy vision of reconciliation, I agreed to meet with her. Minutes later, Mom was at the door.

Her silence was ominous as I climbed into the passenger seat of her silver Oldsmobile 442—a 1980s muscle car unsuited to her tiny physical frame. As we headed downtown, everything seemed just as I'd envisioned: we were on our way toward Dairy Queen. But she made a sudden right-hand turn onto B Street and, a few blocks later, parked the car outside Trinity Baptist Church.

My stomach hurt. This was not going to end well.

I'd had a long love/hate relationship with evangelical Christianity. For years, I spent Sunday mornings listening to sermons from the Baptist preacher—whose favorite theme seemed to be railing about evil homosexuals and how they were doomed to burn forever in the fiery pits of Hell.

We sat together silently in the Church parking lot. Soon she stood outside my door, waiting for me to get out. I didn't know what I was doing back here after a three-year absence. Still the obedient son, trying to please her, I followed her down a narrow, darkly carpeted hall toward the office of the pastor, Rev. Stucky. On our way, we passed icons of Jesus and the Baptismal where, four years earlier, I had been submerged, my soul saved for all eternity.

I imagined the pastor waiting for us, holding a cross to perform some type of Southern Baptist-style exorcism. As we stepped over the threshold to his office, Mom said: "I can't do anything with him."

The painting of Jesus on his wall glared down at me as Mom turned and walked away. My mouth dropped open in disbelief. I had hoped Mom would be a friend, but she had just become an enemy.

As the door to his office closed behind me, it felt as if there were an uncomfortable shift in the space-time continuum. What followed was one of the most humiliating and surreal experiences of my life.

Rev. Stucky stared at me a while. Although he had railed against homosexuals from the pulpit for years, I'm not quite sure he had sat facing a 17-year-old gay boy he had recently baptized.

"Well," he said in his southern drawl, "this is a real disappointment." I don't remember much of anything else he said. I do know he asked me to get on my knees and pray with him while he read select passages from the Bible. He also had me read some sections aloud. He seemed to think we could "pray away the gay".

As he read to me, my mind flashed back to Easter Sundays when, as a very young boy, I emerged from the back of the church into the bright April sunlight. My mother held my hand as she tugged me forward through the crowd. Rev. Stucky and some of the church deacons always stood at the rear of the Church greeting people on their way out.

But the last thing we did, every week before it was time to go, while the collection plates were being circulated, rain or shine, was to sing the hymn "Just as I Am." The hymn was used as a way to encourage people to seek baptism.

Just as I am without one plea,
But that Thy blood was shed for me,
And that Thou bidst me come to Thee,
O Lamb of God, I come, I come.

Just as I am, and waiting not
To rid my soul of one dark blot,
To Thee whose blood can cleanse each spot,
O Lamb of God, I come, I come.

As a young man, I felt like the song dragged on forever. As years passed, I realized I was the only teenager—maybe, the only person in the entire church—who had never been baptized. The peer pressure started to weigh on me. I didn't feel like I had to do anything special in order to make God love me. The day came when I forced myself out of the pew and to the front of the church, as congregants behind me shouted "Amen brother!" and "Save his soul, Lord!" It felt like what was expected of me. The downside was that any time a person came up front during the hymn, the service lasted another 10 minutes.

As I crouched on my knees in his office, I still felt God loved me. My mind wandered as the Pastor finished his endless liturgy of readings, songs and prayers he had prepared to change my attraction to other men. It was pointless to attempt a real conversation.

By this point, I had learned to keep my emotions hidden, as a sort of natural reflex to all the oppression. Years of acting classes came in handy when I figured out how to deal with people who wanted to force their religious judgment on me.

Finally, after an excruciating 90 minutes of supplication, I asked contritely, "Do you think I can call to get a ride home? I have to get up early for finals tomorrow."

"Well son," he said, "do you think that you've taken to heart what we've been talking about?"

"Definitely," I said. That much was absolutely true.

He pointed a bony finger toward the phone. I tried not to appear in too big a rush to call my aunt and uncle, for fear my excitement would cause him to decide I needed to stay even longer.

"Hey, Uncle Ron, do you think you could come pick me up now? I'm at Trinity Baptist."

"What are you doing there?" he asked.

"Oh, I've been having a talk with the Pastor."

"You have?" he asked. "So that's where your mom took you. Yeah, I can be there in a few minutes. I'm leaving right now."

I graduated high school a few weeks later. In another two months, I turned 18. In August, 1979, I filled up my 1967 Buick Special with gasoline and had my high school friend Steve meet me at my parents' house. When I got there, the garage door was wide open. All my things waited for me. No one was home; the door to the house was locked. I couldn't even use the bathroom. I had to pee in the backyard.

I didn't speak to my parents for more than two years after that.

After an internship at KLCC Radio and while I was still in college, I was hired as a news reporter for KPNW AM/FM, a 50,000-watt radio station. It was the most powerful AM station between Seattle and San Francisco. On the first day of my job, the news director took me out for a ride in the news car, and handed me a joint.

"Do you know why I hired you?" he asked.

"Because I'm a good reporter?"

"No! I wanted to be the first radio station in town with an avowed homosexual on the air!"

I didn't even know what the word 'avowed' meant.

Times and sensibilities quickly changed. Two years later, the pot-smoking liberal news director was fired. Soon after, he hooked up with an evangelical girlfriend and made a point of inviting me to visit him so he could tell me, in person, that I was doomed to spend eternity in the fiery pits of Hell.

A few years later, in 1983, at age 22, I began to follow the living Indian guru, Hazur Charan Singh Ji. Until his death, several years later, millions of people around the world believed he was a spokesman for God, much like Jesus.

I became a strict vegetarian and stopped drinking and smoking pot. I was ready to change my diet, and my entire life, to find the meaning I hadn't found from the Baptist church. By 1988, I broke off a four-year relationship and started dating women. I was absolutely sure God would now approve of me, and would soon begin speaking to me directly. In 1990, Charan Singh Ji was succeeded by his nephew, Gurinder Singh.

Over the years, I traveled to India multiple times and for nearly 30 years I meditated an hour or two daily, and waited for God to answer.

It was 1996 when the omnipotent may have appeared in a vision or a blissfully crazy dream. It's impossible to say with certainty that this happened. If the experience *was* real, it taught me that none of us has anything to worry about.

It occurred one afternoon inside a tent, deep in the heart of a compound in northern India known as the Radha Soami Satsang Beas. There were roughly 75 people at the same place. All of us were mentally open to experience the wonderment of God. I sat very still and it seemed as if a bright white light appeared before me.

The pool of white light grew larger, flooding over me and growing in intensity. It radiated with sparkles of many colors, as it overtook everything in the room. Even though I was sitting still, I felt as if I were being pulled into—and floating inside—an endless ocean of love. It felt strangely familiar. Tears of joy streamed down my face as I was filled with the sense that this vision was communicating with me. Its message was that everything happens for a reason.

In that moment I became absolutely sure that this power is with us at all times. We are all a particle of an endless ocean of light. It lasted several minutes, and I felt it was telling me that the time-space we live in exists only so that we may improve ourselves. By improving ourselves, we serve to improve the perfection of God, as beloved droplets of the same flawless, limitless sea.

It is not possible for me to explain the experience further— except to say that it felt like pulsating waves of love coming from a bright white (or colorless) entity, breaking through the visible boundaries of physical space.

Although I don't have proof, I still regard the vision as real. I was fully awake and alert when it happened. It took me years to accept the fact that it may not have been the Guru causing the experience —but rather that it occurred because my mental state was one of complete openness—a state available to anyone willing to attempt it. It seems likely the experience was influenced by my being halfway around the world, in a foreign land free of obligations, worries or cares.

A day or two later, I sat down to collect my thoughts. I had been reading my favorite book, *The Book of Mirdad*. All I can guess is that it influenced my writing style significantly. I was afraid to write about my actual experience; I felt anyone reading it would think I was crazy, though anyone with a similar experience, or mystical inclination, might understand:

> As I enter the room, I look up to notice the stone
> walls, 45 feet high at least, surrounding me. They
> are 50 feet in length and each wall has five windows,
> fifteen feet above the ground, ten feet in height and
> very ornate.

> The windows fill the room with light from every
> direction, as it is bright outside. In fact, it is almost
> as if the walls are there to keep out the light, which
> is so bright that it would blind me if I were to see the
> beloved outside of the hall. The walls are there for
> my protection, even though I may not consciously be
> aware of it.

The room is empty except for my beloved sitting on a chair in the center. The floor is cobblestone, and my eyes sometimes look to the floor out of nervousness or fear. I am not sure exactly which. My beloved's form changes occasionally, but is always human in appearance. Nevertheless, it is always glowing and radiant, also on the verge of blinding but not quite. And the only word I can think of is magnetic beauty. It is so attractive that you can't stand in the doorway and watch. Already as I have written this, I have taken 20 steps forward into the hall.

I look at my beloved and say, "I wish I could have seen you when you looked like this, other than in a dream."

To this he smiled at me and said, "But of course you have. You simply do not remember."

"How cruel a fate this is," I said. "To not remember your beloved's face—even after having seen it so."

"But you have seen me many times since," he said.

And while I knew this to be true, as I had seen and wept with this knowledge on my first passage, it still seemed cruel.

"Yes, yet it is not the same. I feel the same love yet my eyes deny me the pleasure of your sweet irresistible face to which I know there is no cure, no potion, no method of resistance."

"Perhaps that is why you are denied," he said. "Once you have reached the goal, what is the purpose of the search?"

"I should be happy to reach the goal and worry about it then," I replied.

To this he laughed good-humoredly and shook his head.

"My son, I have a place for you already. I have set the dishes on the feasting table myself and I assure you I will see you there. You have a little time yet as I have things for you to learn, and things for you to teach."

"But I have no credentials!" I argued. "I taught one day and you were there watching me fail miserably."

"That was bad," he said. "You misunderstand me though. There are more ways to teach than one."

"Fine," I said, staring into his smiling eyes. "Only promise me it won't be long. This life, though relatively pleasant, and blessed by you with days of fortune and longing, is still a relative hell."

"Oh, to know that you are missing me," he said, "is my greatest treasure. I want you to miss me more!"

"Cruel Master!" I cried.

"No," he said, "not cruel, just another way to get you ready for the feast. Besides, I have to finish setting the table in the other room of the castle. So you must excuse me."

I turned to leave the room and heard the sound of a great wind, yet nothing was blowing. When I turned around to see, both the Master and the chair were gone. I heard his voice echoing in the chamber.

"Before you can eat," he said, "I have to be sure you're really hungry."

In my decades of searching for God, I found that religions were often like well-meaning parents. Many of them might believe they preached acceptance and love, but in their hearts they were judgmental, and imagined themselves the only true path to enlightenment, or heaven.

After I'd spent years running around seeking approval from others, I realized one important truth: the only person I needed approval from was me.

I never imagined having a child, and Rico was a boy who likely never imagined having a gay man as a friend. Undoubtedly we were both learning something important: that accepting each other's faults and differences led to the best of all possible worlds.

If there was something I was going to have to accept about Rico, it was that he moved at his own pace and not mine. Just as my parents had tried to change me, I was coming to accept that there were certain aspects of Rico's personality that I wouldn't change either.

Chapter 30

Year Five: August 2010

It took an entire year to get permissions, fill out paperwork and plan our trip to Germany. Employees of the Oregon Department of Human Services (DHS) sent a raft of emails asking for excruciatingly detailed information about our travels. Each request they sent gave me further resolve to submit every shred of data—plus more! My responses had painstakingly detailed information about air and car travel, hotels, relatives in attendance (including their addresses, phone numbers and emails), and itineraries which detailed nearly everything we'd be doing for every hour of every single day. With my years of experience as a litigation paralegal, I prepared each bit of information as if assembling exhibits for a case going to trial.

By this point, even though it seemed Rico wasn't interested in going with us, I desperately wanted to defeat the paper tiger. I wanted DHS to approve the journey. I wanted to win!

Though every request from the State was answered, I was ultimately forced to give up any hope of taking Rico with us. He hadn't bothered to keep his grades up, and didn't seem to care. When asked, he would say, "Yeah, that's not gonna happen." Though most teens would have wanted a European vacation, Rico was not most teens. I wondered whether his self-esteem was so low he didn't think he was worth it.

On reflection, that seems more than a little naïve. David and I were trying all the things white middle-class people did: to take a trip outside the country, see some sights, enlighten him on how the world really worked and find a deeper emotional bond.

Final score: Paperwork: 1. Aaron: 0.

By this point, Rico had been in the temporary custody of his mother for a full year. Award of temporary custody meant they could still put him back into foster care if things weren't going well.

With another court hearing pending, Rico's caseworker Cindy told me the state was planning to seek permanent dismissal of his case. She planned to recommend awarding full custody to his mother.

Rico's response to being at home with his mother was to give up on himself. His shoplifting, the close call in getting a 14-year-old girl pregnant and his falling grades all occurred immediately after he moved back with his mom and her now two-year-old son, Diego.

I was against the motion to dismiss; in my opinion, Rico needed to be returned to foster care. If the state ended Rico's case, it would close future family counseling that they all still desperately needed. The state was no longer interested in Rico's chances of graduating from high school.

I emailed Cindy protesting the case closure:

> I believe counseling is important to the family and should be mandatory. With three boys under the control of a single parent working full time, she wouldn't have the time to be sure Rico would not be susceptible to gang influences.

Cindy replied:

> Subject: RE: terminating services

> We are pretty limited in what we can do. The services we've provided have not produced any meaningful change. Therefore, it makes little sense to continue providing them in the hopes that eventually somehow there will be an improvement.

...There is simply no evidence to suggest that Mom
will ever benefit, no matter how many services
we offer or for how long. We also have no basis
on which to ask the court for a removal because
there are no imminent safety threats to the children,
even though their long term outcomes are likely
to be much poorer than they would have had they
remained in foster care. The judge can always order
that the children be placed back into foster care if she
feels that is in their best interests.

–Cindy

Rico's therapist, Veronica, supported my argument, and e-mailed
that Rico still needed help from her. She said in part:

Rico is not demonstrating any motivation or
determination to fulfill his responsibilities. He loses
sight of his potential and falls victim to realizing his
mother's shortfalls and gives up on himself.

Rico's mother was in no position to support him, but the Judge
decided it wasn't possible to help in any meaningful way.

The judge opted to close the case, and wrote in the court order:

"Rico is not doing particularly well in his mother's
care. His schoolwork is not being completed and his
grades are below his capability. He has no structure
in the home and his needs are not being met."

Yet she awarded custody to his mother anyway.

Final score: State of Oregon: 0. Rico: 0.

To be fair, the judge *had* wanted to put Rico back in foster care. With no imminent threat to his safety, she claimed to be unable to take action without a request from him. The judge told Rico he had until the following Monday to call her if he decided he wanted to return to foster care.

I wrote to Rico's therapist, Veronica, to let her know he was being given a final chance to return voluntarily to foster care. Veronica had just met with Rico and wrote back:

> Our focus today was primarily on not giving up as seen by Rico's shutting off and relating to his mother on autopilot. He has some homework to do, he has some serious thinking to do about whether he wants to stay with his mother and do his part and the work necessary to make this a healthier relationship or to consider moving back to the stability of what his foster parents can offer.
>
> –Veronica

I called Rico. "I think you should go back," I said. My gut kept telling me he was one bad decision away from self-destruction.

"I'm talking to my mom about it," he replied. He texted later: "I'll be calling the judge on Monday to take care of it."

Saying Goodbye

David and I boarded the plane for Germany, and awaited takeoff. I texted Rico: "Did you call the judge yesterday?"

Rico: "No."

Aaaarrrgh!

I sat back in my seat and closed my eyes. I could feel the tears coming on. Several more nights in a row, I had awoken, overcome with emotion as I fought back a sense of dread and loss of control over Rico's future. He said he was doing his homework, but his teachers told another story. It was wearying to give Rico so much of my time, and feel it wasn't doing any good.

His "lawyer", caseworker and even the judge had all given up on him. The judge had written on the court order that Rico was not doing well with his mother. She knew his needs were not being met. Yet she put him back at home anyway.

His caseworker was tired of his case. His lawyer's interest was in giving Rico what he wanted—not necessarily what was best. Veronica, his counselor, was considered a vendor. Her opinion didn't matter. In legal terms, I was a nobody. Even though I probably knew Rico better than any adult, my relationship with him was purely informal.

In the eyes of the court, I might as well have been a next-door neighbor. So what if I had a Friendship Agreement? Everyone with a legal responsibility to Rico had bailed.

With his foster parents out of the equation, there was no one left to help Rico *but* me. *Big Brother, father, friend—which was I now? Was it even possible to be all things to a boy with so many social disadvantages and emotional scars?*

David's earlier comment replayed in my brain: "You aren't responsible for him. You can sign up for another Little Brother who will appreciate you."

Maybe Rico did need someone different than me. I reminded myself I had options. *I had options?* I felt so lost. With no help from his foster parents, how would Rico survive? His lack of motivation and general apathy had increased. Now the state had cut him loose completely. It could only get worse!

The stewardess made the standard announcements about luggage and the overhead bin. I tried not to look as people walked past. Tears rolled down my face. I was exhausted, and didn't feel strong enough to cope. The endless trail of paperwork had done me in: school releases, releases for activities, releases and ongoing detailed reports to Big Brothers/Big Sisters, the year-long paper trail intended to help Rico get to Germany, my written and actual court testimony and countless phone conversations and emails to Rico's caseworker, therapist, teachers and coaches. They had all been for nothing.

The paperwork, at last, had won out.

I blinked back the tears and stared down at my phone. I slowly typed an email to Rico:

> I can't be your Big Brother anymore. It's just too much. You're being narcissistic and self-centered and not thinking about anyone but yourself. I have spent years doing things with you, yet you never even remember my birthday. You need to get your act together brother. But you will have to do it without me.
>
> This is the end of the line, Rico. I'm sorry.
>
> Goodbye.

Chapter 31

Year Five: Summer - Fall 2010 (11th Grade)

As our flight to Germany got off the ground, we had to power down our phones. The thought of Rico had me feeling fed up. Or so I thought...but I wasn't—not really. Though Rico's life drama had made me cry, the thought of leaving him adrift made me even sadder. I was afraid of what he might do.

Soon, panic set in. I began to think that Rico might try to kill himself. It was easy to picture Rico in an Emergency Room somewhere, all because he thought no one gave a shit. It's the kind of thing Russell might have done. Teenage boys aren't always rational—they can be moody and dark. Rico's family cared, but they thought he was out of control. How could I give up on him, just like all those other adults? How could I leave him? Is that how he would remember me? There was no one left.

Yes he was being narcissistic and self-centered. At that age, I was, too. Yes, he forgot my birthday every year, but whose birthday had I remembered? Yes, he was doing worse at school—but would he do better left alone?

The experience with the white light came back to me. If I was told we were all one, wouldn't abandoning Rico mean I was actually hurting myself?

After hours of mental anguish, we finally had Wi-Fi access. It was the middle of the night in Germany. I sent Rico a text message at 3 pm Oregon time:

> Me: It's after midnight here. I'm sorry I sent you that email. I was feeling really frustrated. It was not appropriate for me to do that.

> Rico: Yeah sure..... Well i don't care. I just hope your happy wit wat ever you do with your life. I really did appreciate everything you and your Families did for me (yours and david'z) for the encouragement and faith you guys had in me. And i'm truly sorry i let EVERYONE down... and Not just that one time.....I did it time and time again.... I just want you to be the best person you can be... And i'll do the same.

> Me: That was not the mature thing to do. but i did it anyway and it wasn't right.

> Rico: Past actions can't be changed. We can only make our futures....

> Me: Well, I care, so I hope that will be good enough, even if you don't.

> Rico: Ok.....

> Me: All right then, let's agree to be better people. I am willing to try if you are.

> Rico: I have nothing to say about that.....

> Me: I want to see you be that better person.

> Rico: Ok. .... And i appreciate that.... But you can't take me the entire way.... You know that too....

Me: I will see you when I get back.

His text messages seemed surprisingly mature for someone who had been so emotionally distant.

Germany was an experience both beautiful and horrifying. David's niece and her fiancé were wed in an old church in Fulda, in the central part of the country. There were many wedding traditions the day of the ceremony. First, the bride and groom used scissors to cut a heart drawn onto a bed sheet. They raced against each other to complete the cut-out—but the wife received a dull pair of scissors, to symbolize how much harder her job would be.

Next the newlyweds set a cage full of doves free. Then, they cut through a log together with a two-handled crosscut blade—as a symbol of the mutual effort required in marriage.

That day of beautiful, uplifting matrimonial symbols was followed, a few days later, by visits to Nuremberg, the Nazi Rally Grounds and the Dachau concentration camp. They were emotionally devastating experiences that left everyone feeling sick and depressed.

Reboot

When I saw Rico, after our return to the U.S. a couple of weeks later, there was no mention of our text messages. That was fine with me—the incident still felt raw. He seemed embarrassed, as if he expected me to disconnect. We were both taking a step back. Perhaps we had to reach the bottom of our relationship before climbing up again.

It turned out we had to pretty much start over.

It seemed as if every past issue we'd had repeated itself, one after another. Rico had told me I wasn't his father, but sometimes treated me like one. He asked me to watch his sports (and bring snacks) but didn't want to talk to me. I had to tell him again, as when he was 12, that he at least needed to say hello.

While his response to my criticism in junior high had been to wander up to me and peep out a meager "hi" before heading for the showers, as a teenager he responded by spending 15-20 minutes talking with me before he wandered off with his snacks and Gatorade. A couple of times he put his arm around my shoulder in a gym full of wrestlers. Once again I found myself feeling uncomfortable—but not for me this time, for *him*. I could only imagine the shit he put up with from his friends about his gay Big Brother.

As Rico matured and spent time talking to and trying to be close to me, I faced a different, unexpected emotion—sadness. Sadness that he was turning into an adult, and that it was happening much too soon.

It had been said, many times, that being a friend was the most important quality when being a Big Brother. My therapist Linda had said: "Just show up and be someone to talk to…they have all kinds of other people telling them what to do…" This brother/mentor/father/friend thing didn't matter so much—it was all about showing up. Trying mattered.

It started to feel as if Rico was working to redefine us, too. It was a continual process.

One night, when it was raining especially hard, I took him home after a movie. The windshield wipers whipped back and forth at top speed as I asked, "Why does it seem like it's always raining when I take you home?"

"Because it's sad that we can't be together," he replied.

At first I was suspicious. *Was he about to ask me for 20 bucks?* He continued: "It's like the time we left bowling and on the way there it was sunny and when we came out it was raining really hard. It was sad that I had to go home."

Role definition

Rico needed to understand what motivated me to become a Big Brother in the first place. One evening, while he visited our apartment, I took a page out of Dad's playbook.

I asked Rico if he'd like to make five bucks in exchange for listening to me talk. He agreed.

"Why do you think I'm volunteering to help you?"

He seemed stumped. "I don't know."

"I do it because I'm trying to do something so I'm not thinking about myself all the time. If all we ever do is think about ourselves and we never think about anyone else, then what good are we?"

He stared at me.

"There are a lot of other things I could be doing with my time. So I wanted you to know why I am spending time with you. I want to help you however I can. I don't believe life is all about the individual. I hope that when you grow up and you're able to, you'll spend some time doing something for others and that you'll be able to pay it forward."

I said the same thing a few different ways. Before I knew it, my five minutes were up. Rico may, or may not, have taken any of it to heart, but I knew he appreciated the five bucks.

The Son

By December, Rico turned 16 and returned to acting out the needy son role. He took the MAX light rail from his house to mine and spent many afternoons/evenings hanging out. It seemed better for him to be in our high rise apartment than sitting at home alone playing videogames—or God knows what else.

Rico called me every time he wanted something—usually money, shoes, or clothes. When we went somewhere together, he often asked me for cash. It was never a large amount: usually $10 or $20. I always asked him what it was for. Sometimes I made him bring me receipts. David didn't want me giving Rico cash because he was afraid he would use it to buy drugs. [I didn't think he was, but later he told me he was going to parties and taking MAX home drunk late at night—throwing up at least once on the train ride home.]

Setting limits for Rico wasn't easy. Like any teenager, he tried to wear me down by asking for something over and over until he got it. I tried to compromise by giving him exactly half of what he wanted. Knowing this was my modus operandi, he likely figured out that the best strategy was to ask for twice as much money as he really wanted.

His nagging inspired a revival of more of my father's lectures. I didn't believe it was always in a child's best interest to buy them whatever they asked for. If kids saw material things as the equivalent of love, they would never be satisfied. We'd already violated our Friendship Agreement: Rico wasn't ever supposed to ask me for money.

I wanted Rico to communicate with me, yet my feelings were bottled up, due to his asking for cash. It had gone on so long that feelings of disengagement returned. I wanted to have a deeper communication with him. I wasn't sure how to get there.

A couple of days later Rico called our house landline.

"Brother! I'm over at Lloyd Center with some friends. I was wondering if you could come over here and loan me 40 dollars so I can buy a pair of shoes?"

I was in an unusually foul mood that day. Rico hadn't figured out my anger management strategy: (a) stuff it inside, (b) stuff it deeper inside, (c) stuff it as far down as possible—(d) EXPLODE!

I had arrived at (d).

"I know you think I wipe my ass with five dollar bills!" I yelled. "I have to work for my money, asshole!" Before I slammed down the receiver I said, "Get a job, Rico! I am not your dad, and I'm not your fucking ATM!"

That was not a stellar Big Brother moment, but it was something he needed to hear. He had made it clear to me he didn't want me for a father—so he had no leeway to treat me like one.

His other mother?

In my highest moments, I stressed the importance of education. My role in this relationship wasn't clear, but Rico started referring to me as his "other mother."

Rico's mother had given me written permission to access to his online school records—and to talk about his progress and problems with school personnel. In late fall of his junior year, his mother and I were called in to meet with one of his school counselors. There was a fantastic new real-time database that gave access to current grades, homework assignments, and instant attendance updates. Electronic monitoring had arrived—and it was every teenager's worst nightmare.

I texted Rico: "I just met with a counselor at your school. We talked about your grades. You have a lot of work to do."

"Thank you for caring," he replied.

Later, as I looked through his attendance record in the online database, it appeared he most often missed his first period science class. Since I lived too far away to wake Rico up for school in person, I signed up for a robocall service. It sent text messages and made calls to his cell phone each morning. I made recordings saying things like: "Get your ass out of bed! It's time to get up and go to class!"

I scheduled texts and phone calls to be delivered at 6 and 6:30 a.m., with other reminders throughout the day.

Rico never mentioned that he was receiving my messages, but I was pretty stoked about them. It felt like I had empowered myself as an omnipresent force from beyond. Perhaps there was a way to join that white light after all.

On the occasional days that I didn't have the energy or desire to hang out with Rico, I went anyway. And each and every time, I left with a full and grateful heart. I focused on reminding Rico that he would need to take care of himself soon. He needed to break free of the cycle of government dependence, uncertainty, and poverty. I explained that I had been on food stamps while in college, but wasn't embarrassed about it, because it was clear I'd pay plenty of taxes after I got out. I wanted Rico to imagine his successful future.

To focus Rico's vision, I reiterated the four options drummed into my head by my father: he would have to get an education, marry for money, develop a talent, or inherit money. One thing was certain: neither Rico nor I were set to inherit cash.

The missing piece

Though Rico had my full support, whenever the topic of fatherhood came up in homework, his sadness was evident. In one assignment, he was to read the first several pages of a story before writing a conclusion in the form of a three-minute play. The story began with a boy and his father living in a world of cannibals. One night, as they huddled outdoors in sub-freezing weather, the father tried to encourage his son by telling him that everything would be all right. Trying to stay warm, the son fell asleep holding onto his father. When he woke the next morning, the boy was shocked to find that his father had died and left him completely alone in the forest.

In Rico's ending, the son passed several days carrying on a conversation with the corpse, as he waited for someone to rescue him. During that time he told his father how much he missed him, and how he wished they could still be together. Eventually the boy left to live with the family of a friendly passer-by.

It seemed a metaphor for his relationship with his real-life father. His dad was dead to him, but he made do with the kindness of strangers. It made me wonder how many nights in Rico's boyhood he had talked to his absent father, hoping for his eventual return.

Chapter 32

Year Five: November 2010 (11ᵗʰ Grade)

Early one November morning, at my parents', Rico and I stood next to each other at double sinks in the master bath. Our faces were covered in shaving cream. I handed him a razor so he could try shaving for the first time. As I looked into the mirror at our reflections. Time seemed to slow down. Thoughts about yesterday, or what would come later that day, or what I had planned for tomorrow ceased. It was not a scene I could have ever imagined.

Rico stood next to me, waiting.

At the sight of his face, I felt a sudden surge of emotion. *Where was the little boy? Where had he gone?* I turned away from the mirror and tried not to cry. Like my parents, I was raised to avoid showing emotion; whatever this feeling was discomforted me. Looking back on this moment, my only regret is that I didn't break down and cry, so I would have had to explain it to him.

Rico held his razor to his cheek, awaiting instructions. "Uh… ok, now what?" He asked, "Uh—what are you doing?"

"Just let the shaving cream sit there a minute." I wiped my eyes, took a deep breath and turned around. "Okay. Watch me."

The razor might have been disposable, but this moment would remain burned into my brain forever.

Big Brother/Big Impact?

That same month, Rico and I enjoyed our 15 minutes of fame.

Big Brothers/Big Sisters had their annual fundraising breakfast. As a member of the agency's Ambassador Board, I wanted to get the gay and lesbian community to get more involved. It was likely that many of them had difficult childhood experiences, and could empathize with at-risk youth. I wrote the local LGBT paper *Just Out*.

At this same time, the controversy over discrimination against gays in the Boy Scouts was in the headlines. A *Just Out* reporter contacted me, and a story appeared in November 2010 edition under the headline "Gay Mentor Teaches Tolerance—Big Brother, Big Impact."

It read in part:

> His brotherly relationship and its attendant culture clashes have not only helped Rico perform better in school and eschew affiliation with Latino gangs, they have influenced him to be accepting of differences.
>
> Despite the differences between the two, it is clear that Rico has a respect for his mentor that he might not have had for gay men otherwise. Rico has even stood up for him to his mother and peers. A youth who could have echoed the attitudes of his family and peers and become a bully now defends someone who, in another time and place, could have been a victim.

Soon after the article appeared, Rico and I learned we had been nominated for national Big & Little Brother of the year. We were told it could mean a trip to the White House to meet with President Obama.

In order to compete, we each had to write 400 word essays.

My Statement:

I have been a Big Brother for over four years. My Little Brother Rico was a 7th grader and 12 years old when we met.

I know that my Little Brother once lay in bed at night awake, in foster care, hoping for someone besides his foster parents to be part of his life. Not someone to be his parent, but someone to be a friend.

Our first visits were spent riding bikes, playing Frisbee in the park, hiking, and if it was raining, going to a movie or the arcade.

Over the past four plus years I have done many of the things Rico likes to do, but I have also tried to broaden his horizons by taking him with me to places he would never otherwise visit. This includes talking with the Rabbi at my synagogue, watching the musical "Guys and Dolls" at Portland Center Stage, and two years ago attending to a lecture in Portland by Supreme Court Justice Ruth Bader Ginsburg. Last summer, we went on his first airplane ride.

We have visited my parents a few times together.
As it turns out they are the closest thing he has to
grandparents.

But that's just the stuff, right? The things you do with
youth when you're trying to get to know them; get
them to open up and see what life has to offer; and try
to be a Big Brother to them.

It hasn't all been smooth sailing. There have been
times when I felt his family issues and his own
behavior were too much for me to handle. It's an
investment of both time and your emotional self.

It was after our third visit that I realized it wasn't
me that was changing his life, but rather, that he
was changing mine. He forced me to set time aside
for mentoring, and our visits often turned back my
mental clock to consider the feelings and fears I had
at his age.

My mind often travels forward in time. I wonder
whether he will one day be a doctor like he says
he wants to be. I wonder if he will join the Navy
right out of high school so he can use the welding
skills he's developed. I wonder if he'll have a wife
and children and what kind of life they will have.
I wonder if I will be around to see all these things.
And I wonder whether anything I have done has
influenced his path to adulthood and self-sufficiency.
I know that these are the things I may not know for
years to come.

Today a thousand children wait for the same opportunity. They hope for someone to spend a few hours with them every week or two, something they can look forward to in their lives, someone to give them direction, and hope for the future.

Rico's Statement:

Had I not met Aaron, my life could have ended up in many different ways. None is for certain though, given that I am his little brother. In many ways, I believe I probably would've ended up in some sort of gang, or behind bars, I say this because where I was living wasn't exactly the best side of town and a lot of the gangs of my nationality came from the area.

Before Aaron, I used to dress like any typical gangster, baggy clothes, mostly all one color and didn't care for school. When I met him I was in foster care, and didn't feel like I was getting the support I needed at the time. After I did, he pushed me to focus on school, showing me how crucial it is to graduate, how grades and the people in school could help or hurt me.

When I started foster care I was starting middle school, and as many people know, these years are the hardest for most kids/young adults. Aaron came into my life after my first year of foster care, and we weren't really all that close. In reality, you can't get close to someone you have just met. I thought he was a decent guy and very optimistic. At the beginning we weren't really on the same level of looking at the world, he looked at it as if it had options and I felt like it was horrible and life is all full of mistakes.

At first people probably looked at us as what are they doing together? But now, we've gotten past that and ignore the staring. We have moved on and keep our lives together as brothers should. We enjoy our time and support each other when we need it, but we don't let my language barrier get in the way. Knowing me has made him want to learn Spanish and learn another culture to its full extent. We've both have met the others family and both sides enjoy the others company as family.

Aaron has been in my life long enough he's seen me grow a foot, change my voice and grow a beard. Till this day, I don't regret accepting him as my big brother. We have known each other long enough that each of our friends recognizes the other one as his brother.

–Rico

Rico's letter told me more about how he felt about our relationship than anything he ever said to me.

Apparently Rico's Air Jordans upset his nine-year-old brother, Luis. He was jealous of our time together. One day, as we were bowling, Rico said, "my brother notices I have nice clothes and he likes my Nintendo games. Do you think you could buy him a few things?"

Luis was recently returned to his mother's home from foster care. The moment tugged at my heartstrings. There were thousands of boys like Rico, including his brother, and their infant brother Diego. I wanted to be able to help more young men like Rico, but couldn't help them all. I had only seen Rico's little brother a handful of times the past four years... and we didn't have a Friendship Agreement.

I did think Luis might be a good little brother for David, and asked Rico to bring Luis to a movie. Luis wanted to see *Diary of a Wimpy Kid*. I asked David to come along.

While we waited for the movie to start, Rico pointed to my temple and exclaimed, "I see a gray hair!"

"Yeah," I replied, "and you're the one who gave it to me!"

Afterward, we all went bowling. Luis kept right up with David while Rico and I walked behind at a slower pace.

"Look at them. They walk exactly the same!" said Rico.

David had been thinking about becoming a Big Brother. As Rico and I walked to the register to order our bowling shoes, Luis grew serious. He asked David, "Are you looking for a Little?"

"Yes I am!" David said.

Luis seemed a little surprised and replied in a half-whisper, "I'm looking, too!"

As David paid the bill, Luis stood next to him, his chin barely reaching the top of the counter. He looked up at David and asked innocently, "Are you rich?"

In his eyes we were most definitely rich.

David and Luis were officially matched as Big and Little brothers a few weeks later, on March 11, 2011.

Chapter 33
Girls, Cars, and Work

Girls

Rico started treating me differently. He talked to me about girls. One evening he got a call from a friend as we headed to his home:

"I asked her—not direct like—was she goin' to the dance? And she said she was going, yeah—with her brother and some of her girlfriends! So later, I asked her brother, straight up, 'was she goin' or should I ask her?' And he said, 'yeah, you might as well ask her, cuz what's the worst thing that could happen… she could say no!' So on Monday I'm gonna have an assignment…" And then in a high squeaky voice he added "nerrrrr-vous!"

Rico's conversation was amusing; I wanted to laugh. I had been munching on some almonds. One of them got stuck in my throat, and led to an uncontrollable coughing spell. Rico said goodbye to his friend on the phone and stared at me.

"So… what part of that do you want to say something about?" he asked. "What is it? What do you want to say to me?"

My eyes watered as I shook my head and choked out, "I don't—I don't have anything to say right now."

Rico waited briefly. "You must have some kind of advice… or something you want to say to me about that?"

"I have no comment on that, really, no," I said, still choking.

"You always have something to say!"

I wasn't even sure which girl he was talking about.

I swallowed and said, "When we first met, you seemed depressed and kind of morose."

"What does morose mean?"

"It means sad or gloomy."

"I think I had low self-esteem. I worried a lot that girls wouldn't think I was good-looking. But I'm happier now 'cuz they think I'm a player."

He still depended on others for his self-approval. Somehow we'd have to fix that.

Rico went to the Prom with Mary Lynn. It had been nerve-wracking for him. He told me they had decided they wanted to go steady, and said her dad was especially old-fashioned.

"Why don't you act like a gentleman and ask her dad for permission to go out with her?" I asked.

"When should I ask?"

"At the end of prom night."

"Did you and David like her?"

"Sure, we thought she was great. She's smart and beautiful." I decided to rib him a little bit. "I can't believe you got her to date you. How did you manage that?"

"Does that mean you don't think I'm good enough for her?

"No, that's not what I meant. But she looks like a princess. If you want to date a princess, you have to be a prince!"

For several weeks after that, Rico was the happiest I had ever seen him. He seemed to enjoy the idea of having a steady girlfriend, and acting so public and formal.

"So how's Mary Lynn?" I asked when I picked him up from work one evening.

"We're done, I guess. She broke up with me on Tuesday and changed her Facebook status to 'single.' I feel stupid. My status still says we are in a relationship. Can we stop at your house so I can use your computer?"

"Do you want to talk about it?"

"I knew you were going to ask me that."

On the way to our apartment it was obvious that Rico felt anxious. Out of the corner of my eye, I could see that he was trying not to cry. This was a difficult experience for him. Breakups were especially hard at that age.

"You know," I said, "you shouldn't say anything bad about her to your friends, because she will be the first person to find out."

"Yeah, I figured that out because she is already talking about me."

We stopped by my apartment so he could change his Facebook relationship status. I stuck a bowl of pistachios in front of him. He stared at them and said: "I don't want to look at those. It's the same bowl I snacked on when she was here with me."

He signed onto his Facebook page, changed his status to 'single,' and blocked her profile.

"So—why did she break up with you, again?" I asked.

"She said I didn't talk enough about my feelings," he said. "She went back to her old boyfriend."

Ugh. That was the worst.

A few months earlier, I had received a handout from a Big Brothers/Big Sisters workshop about relationships.

"You might want to read this," I said.

I had tried to give him the booklet once before, but he wasn't interested. This time he kept it. "You know," I said, "pretty much any girl will want you to be able to talk about your feelings."

"I don't think I should be measured by that. I think that a girl should look at me like a quarterback, and judge me by how I might shine through during my darkest hour."

Given that in his darkest hour he had wanted to abort a child that could have been his, Rico's philosophy seemed inconsistent. It made me wonder: if someone only knew us during our real, actual worst times, would really want to know us? It seemed more important that we should be judged by whether those experiences actually teach us something.

We got in the car. On the way home, Rico didn't talk at all. As I pulled up to drop him off, he flipped through the document I had given him. "Do you think I should still talk to her?" he asked.

"Yes, you should, because she might realize you were the best thing that ever happened to her." He pressed his lips together really hard, stifled a sob, and sat still a few seconds before opening the car door.

"Okay, that's what I wanted to know," he said as he climbed out.

Cars

Rico's girl trouble heightened his interest in the two other loves of his life: video games, and cars.

He had his first real car when he was 16. His mother swapped her lawnmower for a friend's auto. She told Rico he could have it when he got a license. Rico found the keys and decided to go for a spin. After a few blocks, a police officer spotted his expired plates and pulled him over. Rico had no registration, no driver's license and no insurance. When he explained that he was out for a joyride in his own car, the officer ordered the car towed. He gave Rico citations for driving without a license and insurance. Because no one in his family had $300 for the impound fees, the car was sold for scrap. He never saw it again.

The incident reminded me of my own joyriding days. I was just 15 when I took Mom's car out for a ride. One day while she sat in the car, I'd secretly had an extra key made at a drug store. My own joyriding days came to a halt after the police showed up at our house, looking for me. As it turned out, I wasn't too good at parking, and had a little hit-and-run in the parking lot of the U.S. Bank on Mohawk Boulevard.

Fortunately, the owner was satisfied with a cash payment for the damage; I was never charged.

What would the outcome would have been if I were Latino?

Work

Over the summer, we learned about a special youth employment program. A local hospital was accepting summer interns—specifically from Rico's high school. Rico applied and soon had his first job, working in a medical records department. With overtime, he was pulling in $1,500 a month—even more than his mother.

Rico managed to show up for work on time without too much prompting. The job required measurable output, and his supervisor did regular check on the quantity and quality of his work.

After a co-worker complained Rico was texting and watching Japanese anime on the job, we had a long talk about the kind of behavior that was expected at the office. He apologized to his boss.

I hadn't been a perfect employee, either, so it was difficult for me to be too hard on Rico. In one of my first jobs, at a Dairy Queen, I called in sick one day to go water skiing with friends. I was caught and immediately fired.

From the beginning of his junior year of school, I had paid for Rico's home Internet access. It served as a tool to reinforce good behavior. Over time, I had shut Rico's Internet off and on so many times, for grade and attendance issues, that I completely lost track.

"You know what slacking off at work means, right?" I asked.

"No."

"I'm shutting off your Internet for a while."

"I thought I just had to do well in school!"

I made a point of giving Rico the opportunity to earn his Internet back. The Big Brothers/Big Sisters staff found out about my Internet incentive program, and I learned through the grapevine that some of the match specialists didn't like it. So what? It only cost me $10 a month, and was surprisingly effective.

One day Rico said to me, "I think I'd like to get a job like my friends. You know, working at Taco Bell or Dutch Brothers coffee."

"Sure, you can do that," I replied sarcastically, "if you want to give up your health insurance, vacation days, and retirement plan. Why don't you do that? Why don't you stop making $15 an hour and work for minimum wage at Taco Bell on an irregular night and weekend schedule instead? That sounds great."

At dinner, Rico revealed that he didn't really want to change jobs, but was having difficulty coping with the content.

Maria had made us an amazing dinner of enchiladas. As we ate, Rico looked at me seriously. He put his hand on my shoulder and looked right into my eyes—something he had almost never done.

"I saw some records today about a guy who wanted to commit suicide. That really bothered me a lot."

I wondered what might have brought this on. Maybe the veteran he was talking about was gay? It seemed like he was saying that he'd be upset if I ever decided to kill myself. It reminded me of the night Russell paid me a visit to talk about his gay uncle.

Rico didn't need to worry about me. I was not ready to leave the stage of life on my own.

Chapter 34

Year Six:
Fall 2011 (12th Grade)

Naval Plans

Rico had been talking to Navy recruiters off and on, so the summer before his senior year I took him to the local recruiting station for a visit. He met with a regional recruiting supervisor and a former Navy SEAL. Although Rico had fantasies about being a SEAL, the realities of living in Afghanistan facing sniper fire, or treading water for 12 hours in freezing temperatures, eventually lost its appeal. Apparently, reality didn't live up to videogames or the movies.

The Navy recruiters stressed that Rico needed a clean police record, good grades, and an on-time high school graduation —they would not take a GED. The recruiters encouraged Rico to participate in athletics and said he should also start swimming. They warned him to stay away from drugs and alcohol.

Before I knew it, Rico had begun his final year of high school. He was already working on a paper. His subject was freedom. With summer over, I saw a marked change in his attitude. He had to decide whether to do the work to graduate or not. He realized that if he didn't graduate, it would be his own fault. It impressed me that he seemed to be finally taking responsibility for himself.

Freedom

There is more than one way to look at freedom. Some say freedom is automatic in the choices that are given to you; others say you have to work to earn it. But I would say freedom is a balance between the two things.

Freedom is always there, but how much of it you actually use or get to use depends on the circumstances. I sincerely believe that freedom is partially a state of mind but also partially given to you by someone else because in life there is always someone above you—whether that's a cop, your boss, or your parent. And usually this person is in some way in charge of you and/or your well-being.

Freedom is choice and by choice I mean it gives potential to you. For instance, some people think just because their parents say they are allowed to come home late, it is okay to be irresponsible. In reality, it is not, but some or even most young adults would ignore their common sense and follow their adrenaline rush. Abusing one's freedom could result in the loss of some, most, and/or all of their former freedom.

This can happen for many reasons, but to me it could be because they could not be trusted.

In another example, everyone is free to drive at their own (somewhat) recommended speed. The reason there are speedometers and police officers checking for speeding is because someone at some time tried to push their freedom to its max and may have been sued for causing the death of someone. Being irresponsible like that could result in higher insurance or them losing their vehicle. Like I mentioned, freedom is there. You just have to work for it. I heartily believe that freedom and responsibility go hand in hand. The more freedom you have the more responsibility you have.

The irony of the paper was that his actions at home could be far different. As his sister told me in an email soon after:

So I just spoke to my mom and she says that she had a talk with Rico about responsibilitys [sic] last night and she's glad that you shut off the Internet. She is going to make Rico help pay a bill or two around the house because he has no priorities or want to help himself with having a good job and keeping it, so far everything has been handed to him.

My mom thinks you should have him help you out
with paying for the internet but also let him know
that you will still shut it off if he's not doing what
he needs to be and following rules. Lately he's been
into arguing, or getting mad at my mom if she
tells him something about his gaming station. The
minute he wakes up he starts playing and doesn't
do anything else and I mean nothing. My mom and
I hope that you can motivate him and talk to him
since he back talks and argues with everybody else.

Every adult in Rico's life was encouraging him to apply himself. David even said he would buy Rico a car if he got all As his senior year.

"I'm thinking of taking David up on his offer, and working really, really hard in school this year so I can get a car," said Rico.

"Oh? What kind of car is that?"

"I was thinking maybe a Lamborghini."

"Oh, right! You see that I'm driving a 10-year-old Saab don't you? Maybe you should consider a used Pinto or a Pacer."

"What's a Pinto?"

"Never mind. You need to understand that if David buys you a car, it's not going to be a brand new sports car."

A couple of weeks later, shortly before his internship at the hospital was slated to end, Rico worked on a homework assignment dealing with immigration. We worked together on his PowerPoint project. He became angry in response to something I said.

"You don't understand what it feels like to be Latino and not have any legal rights. I've grown up afraid that my mother would be taken away and deported."

I was surprised he seemed so clueless about my life. Being gay sure had its share of legal drawbacks. After some thought, it seemed he was old enough to appreciate a robust contrasting argument.

That night, I created a spreadsheet to organize my thoughts. I picked him up from home to take him to work early the next morning. It was raining.

As he got out of the car, I handed him my spreadsheet. [Figure 1.]

"Here. I was thinking about what you said yesterday and I thought it would be good for you to take a look at this. I think I actually do know a little about how you feel."

As I drove away, Rico stood in the rain and stared down at my paper. A feeling of guilt came over me. Although I had faced fears, prejudice, and injustice growing up, I didn't think my worst fear could compare to worrying that the government might deport my mother. I thought my teen years were bad, but I was coming to the realization that Rico's were even worse.

Fifteen minutes later I sent him a text message. "I'm sorry. I know it's not the same, but it's not like immigrants are the only people with problems with our government. I wanted you to see that."

Despite my trepidations, this felt like a groundbreaking experience. Would I finally be able to level with Rico like a friend? Wouldn't a friend try to educate another friend about the social consequences of being gay—an area of life that he might not know about?

With Russell, I had just tried to live life as a functional human being and a friend. Today, Microsoft Excel spreadsheets, and years of experience, provided amazing powerful opportunity for specificity. In the decades since high school, life had become more than right or wrong. Like our relationship, life was complicated.

It was important to me that Rico understand it was important to try to understand people, and to think about them within the sphere of their own experiences. Just like my father's, and Russell's, Rico's world was so different from mine that I would never fully comprehend it. My hope was that, by offering insight into my own life, he could learn to have compassion and empathy for others' points of view.

My study of spirituality, and my own experience, had taught me that both we humans and the Supreme Being were continuously evolving for the better.

Despite my attempts to think about our relationship from a high-level perspective, reality always seemed to return abruptly. Before I knew it, Rico's hospital internship came to an end.

Figure 1

Item	Gays	Undocumented Immigrants
Your children can be taken away and you can be deported with or without them, depending on their parentage and citizenship		X
You are forbidden to serve in the military	(until 2011)	X
Being who you are is illegal and you could go to jail	millions of citizens "illegal" until 1972 in Oregon and 1982 nationwide because of statutes about sex	millions of people "illegal"
Living in a town where some people would like to do you physical harm	X	X
"Friends" who stop speaking to you once they find out the "truth" about you	X	X
People fight on TV about whether you should have any legal rights, and people vote on your right to freedom. Your identity is always on TV and in the news.	X	X
Hitler would have had you executed	X	X
Kids at school make fun of you because you are different	X	X (depends on the school)
People in public places look at you funny because you look or act differently	X	X
You may live in fear of being discovered	X	X

Item	Gays	Undocumented Immigrants
Some people think you should not have the right to adopt or have children in America	X	X
Parents try to "cure you" by taking you to psychologists, psychiatrists, ministers or other religious figures	X	
Parents who tell you that you should never have been born	X	
You are not allowed to donate blood to the Red Cross because it might be contaminated, even though they have tests that can show whether or not it actually is and even though you could just as easily have AIDS if you are heterosexual.	X	
Religious figures and others tell you that you are going to burn in hell for all eternity	X	
Parents may be more concerned about what their friends will think of them than anything else	X	
"Being found out" can cost your job -- you can lose your source of income and employment	currently legal to fire people for being gay in 30 states	currently legal to fire people for being illegal in 50 states
Bullied at school by others	X	??
Described as evil, "a problem" and part of an ongoing Political discussion	X	X
Negatively portrayed in the mainstream media	X	X

Chapter 35

Spring 2012: Graduation?

Once his internship ended, Rico began to skip classes even more. It soon became clear he wouldn't have enough credits to graduate. I sent a panicked email to my match support specialist:

> Hi Ellen —
>
> Well...things are worse than I thought on the school front. Rico's mother and I went to see a school counselor yesterday because Rico's mid-term grade report indicated he was failing half his classes.
>
> His mother may be losing her job soon; her company is being sold to a conglomerate that will probably lay her off. Rico may need to go back to work to help support the family.
>
> Rico's wrestling coach is the instructor giving him an "F" in American Government for all his class absences. I asked for his help. I said I knew that Rico looked up to him, and that it would be really helpful to me if he could get Rico to finish school.

The coach wrote back a nice note and then made Rico sit and do homework instead of practice because he hadn't gotten it all done. When I called Rico tonight he blamed me for causing turmoil in his life.

I seriously don't know what else to do. He is really right on the verge of completely failing high school. He has to pass every single class that he has this term, and he has an astronomical 101 unexcused class absences (no joke) and 28 times tardy.

Do you think you could check in with him? I am happy to encourage him all I can and I don't want to give up on him, but it feels like he's given up on himself; and there is not much I can do about that.

–Aaron

The coach had a real impact on Rico. He made him carry around a progress slip—and have it signed daily by all his teachers.

Rico officially signed the paperwork for the Navy. He was accepted, pending his official high school graduation. When he realized he was two credits shy of finishing on-time, he called to ask for my help. He needed money for a college night class. To my surprise, he ended up attending every class on time. One of his projects was a persuasive essay.

Persuasive Essay

Most everyone would agree that losing a loved one is horrible. It is not what we would want from anyone we care about, even our elders when their time comes. So why allow the massacre of innocent children who have not even learned to crawl, talk, and live a life? Abortion is an inconsiderate act and should not be allowed. Everyone deserves the right to this world, no one else should be allowed to make that choice.

When making the choice of abortion, the mother is left with a major decision. The matter of whether or not to lose a life is difficult. Many women cannot cope with this decision and are mentally haunted. Some become severely depressed with regret about the decision. The decision to abort a child is needlessly compounded with complications.

In life one can say "sorry" to help ease the pain from emotional or physical damage. Change can be for the better, but not being able to undo is a different matter and life taking is undoable. However, when a life is gone, there is no return for that child. Some argue rape is the reason why they do not want to have their child; putting the child up for adoption is a better choice. The baby's point of view might be "have I ever done any harm? I deserve a chance at life."

Being holy people, we are going against our faith
and one of the Ten Commandments God gave us,
because abortion is murder. Partaking in this action
is also considered murder in the eyes of God. If we
are to ever be accepted by God, we might as well
accept our fate and appreciate it. If we are to be seen
as followers of God we cannot have this in our hands.
We should be in support of eliminating the law that
allows women to have abortions.

In accepting our choices, we should also accept the
outcomes. Babies are sometimes the outcomes of
the choices we make and abortions should not be
an option. It is easier to prevent occurrence before
it happens, this way there is nothing wrong; no
life was lost. Lives are not toys and should not be
payable, it is very dear and cannot be returned. Some
people today would not be around if their parents
had aborted them, this could have even possibly
prevented our very own existence.

Though impressed by his logic and arguments, I was taken aback.
When he had almost become a teenage father, he had strenuously
advocated for abortion. Now he was against it?

I remembered how traumatized he had been, years earlier, when
he saw the abortion exhibit at the science center. His reasoning still
puzzled me. Did he reconsider his position in light of the paternity
scare?

Perhaps he feared that, had his own mother favored abortion, he might never have been born. She had been fortunate to find the means to raise him.

Rico earned the credit he needed to graduate.

Chapter 36

Match Closure

June, 2012

Big Brother and Big Sister matches officially end when the Little turns 18 or graduates from high school—whichever happens last. Our match would officially close on graduation night.

While I was tremendously relieved that Rico had made it, I was suddenly angry at men like his father, who had left his mother to raise him all on her own.

A week before Rico's official ceremony, Big Brothers/Big Sisters called me about a documentary project that would feature young men writing and reading private letters to their dads. They were looking for one boy who didn't have a dad, but a Big Brother instead.

In my interview I said:

> "It's really sad when a father abandons his child. It's devastating to them. I think people don't really imagine what the consequences of that are. But the lack of self-confidence that they have as a result, and the ongoing damage it does to someone, is inestimable. I think boys really need to have male role models in their life— even if it's not the perfect male role model that they might want to have—it's somebody who wants to get to know them and be a friend.

"There have been times when it's been difficult for me because he had some issues that any teenager would have—things that I did when I was a teenager that he also did. It's just that I got away with them and he got caught. So—all of those feelings that you have as an adolescent—you start to see these young people going through those same things, and you remember what that was like. I had a tremendous amount of empathy for him.

"What surprised me was that I didn't realize how attached he would become. I have become attached to him as well. There are certain things he says now and then that make me realize—"oh that's right, he doesn't have a dad—he has me!"

I was not in the room when Rico read his letter, which said:

"I acknowledge that throughout the years people have come and gone out of my life. Aaron, however, has been there through everything in my life since we first met. There are not many words I can say about our relationship; just that it is equal to a regular sibling one, father and son. We have our disagreements, but through it all you support me in anything I do or have plans to do.

"We have made many memories over the last six years, and some are experiences I may not have had and I just want to thank you for it."

And So It Ends

Rico's graduation ceremony was at the historic Veterans' Memorial Coliseum at Portland's Rose Quarter. The Coliseum holds 13,000 people; it was really full that night. Months earlier, the thought of Rico's graduation left me teary-eyed. By the time it arrived, it felt strangely anticlimactic. I was happy for him, but completely exhausted.

From high in the bleachers, I watched Rico among the nearly 400 graduating seniors. His childhood and teenage years had sometimes been a long and arduous journey. Now that Rico was graduating and would head into the Navy in the fall, I felt proud—like any father.

Yet my relationship with him was officially over.

After we had our photo taken together, I reverted back to my old habits, and lost some ground we had gained.

I didn't tell him I loved him. Or that I would miss him.

Then, just like my father might have done with me, I casually pushed him away, and wished him good night.

Chapter 37

Back at the Ranch House: Summer 2012

On a hot summer day, my parents and I attended a family reunion at a cousin's farm.

Mom and Dad were growing feeble. The first order of business, in delivering my parents to my cousin's, was to plan how to get my 82-year-old, completely blind father to the car. Mother was still able to help dad get around by herself, despite her disfiguring and painful rheumatoid arthritis. But as long as I was visiting them, I wanted to help.

The first step was to help Dad on the long walk from his comfy La-Z-Boy, past the sofa, the TV, through the dining room, down two steps to the den, through the garage and then across the driveway into the car. This 40-yard trek could seem like a quarter mile.

After we arrived at the party, I led Dad to a shady spot so he could sit and talk loudly with others—including my brother. My sister and her wife were busy chatting up our nearly 20 cousins. Over the next few minutes I moved around the tables to visit as many relatives as possible. It wouldn't be long before Mom and Dad wilted in the 90-degree heat. Many of my cousins had not been home in several years. Who knew when I might have a chance to see them again?

Within an hour it was over 90. Someone on the lawn shouted, "He's mobile! Uncle Bob's moving!" I was startled, and headed off toward Dad.

Dad had decided it was time to go. He stood up, wobbling with his arms out in front of him like a zombie. It seemed as if, despite his blindness, he was going to march off somewhere.

He shuddered as I grabbed his arm. Whenever he stood up quickly, it was common for his blood pressure to drop precipitously, which set him up for a fall. He had tripped in the living room, while getting up from his La-Z-Boy, and hit his head several times in the past few months. His doctors warned that the next fall could be his last.

Mom and Dad's car had been in the direct sun for about an hour. The door handles were blistering hot. I sat Dad in the car.

"Let's go!" he said irritably.

I fired up the Buick LeSabre and turned the air conditioning up full blast. It sure seemed like one of us would pass out—either from heat or stress.

Mom posed for one last photo with her four younger brothers in the shade of a giant oak tree. I rolled up alongside them in the car and ushered her to her seat as soon as they were done. Twenty minutes later we were home, and I cranked up the air conditioner while I positioned Dad in his La-Z-Boy. I poured them each a big glass of ice water, and heaved a sigh of relief that we had made it home safely.

Suddenly, I heard the sound of water running somewhere in the house and searched for the source. The usual culprit was a toilet acting up; this time there was a broken sprinkler pipe out back. The dial on the water meter spun wildly as gallon after gallon spewed out. I quickly shut off the water main and went inside.

Mom stood in the kitchen. Dad reclined peacefully in his La-Z-Boy. Neither heard a thing.

"There's a broken pipe in the backyard!" I yelled.

"What?" hollered Dad, fiddling with his hearing aid.

I yelled louder, "You've got a broken pipe!"

Still adjusting his earpiece, Dad yelled back, "I've got what?"

Mom was standing a few feet away, and screamed at the top of her lungs, "He said there's a broken pipe, *Bob*!"

I laughed to see that my 80-something parents, who once held whisper-fights behind closed doors, had taken the gloves off. It was difficult for me to tell whether they yelled out of frustration, exhaustion or anger. This behavior had grown in frequency. If this were part of their transition to treating me more like a friend, I wasn't sure I liked it. Dad alternated between barking orders and scratching his head in an effort to remember where he had buried the sprinkler shut-off valve.

Mom scrambled around the house trying to find a certain scrap of paper she knew had the name of the sprinkler maintenance guy. Pulling out desk drawers crammed with bills and papers, she flipped haphazardly through address books.

Suddenly she stopped and said, "I completely forgot what I was looking for."

As all this happened, Mom's Chihuahua ran up to my ankles and started barking. It was clear why my parents were so panic-stricken. Shutting off water to the house of two 80-year-olds created a crazy sense of urgency. In just seven minutes, my parents' lives had gone from orderly to anarchic.

Three hours later, after a plumber repaired the damage, all was well.

Dad thanked me over and over again, and said he didn't know what he would have done without me. I appreciated the fact that he finally seemed to respect me, if not fully understand me. He told me again how much he really liked David. Dad had come a long way since 1979.

The next day, Russell sent me a text message. He had gotten out of prison a few months earlier, and wanted to get together.

I realized it had been 20 years since I last saw him face-to-face.

Russell, Redux

All through Russell's teen years, and into his 20s, I had probably known him better than anyone. The thought of seeing him again made me more nervous than I anticipated.

He had been married and divorced four times, and imprisoned twice. He'd gone through rehab multiple times. In all those years, I had seen just one newer photo of him. Would I would even recognize him?

We met at Addi's Diner, at South A and Main streets in Springfield. It was my parents' favorite restaurant. The sun shone through the window into the orange vinyl booth as we ate. Russell smiled a lot. He still had a square jaw, and a dimpled chin that amplified his devilish smile.

He had always been a strong man, but today he seemed weaker, even fragile. His laughter was still warm and caring.

Russell told me he was constructing a house and living with his parents upriver. As he spoke, I couldn't help but wonder what he had thought about every day, year after year, in prison. His rap sheet contained counts of forgery, robbery, trafficking in stolen property, burglary and car theft. All this behavior was drug-induced. This wasn't the Russell I knew.

Though he had been through alcohol treatment, he complained about fighting with his parents if he wanted a couple of beers.

As I sipped my orange juice and squirted big blobs of ketchup on my home fries, he explained that he'd placed his future wholeheartedly in the Lord. No money. No retirement. No friends. He was on speaking terms with his 20-year-old son, but his daughter wouldn't have anything to do with him.

"I don't know what I'm going to do when this job ends," he said. "I'm saving up my money to buy a truck to look for work. I also have to buy an interlock device because of my three driving under the influence/DUI charges. That doesn't seem fair. I can't believe the government is making me do that...considering all the other people I know who are out drinking and driving all the time," he said. "Why are they picking on me?"

Because Russell had been in my life, I learned how to be a friend to Rico. Russell taught me how to love without giving up hope when things got tough. If he hadn't been there, I don't think I would have stuck with Rico.

While Russell would always be the high school quarterback who saved my life, Rico would always be the kid who helped me forgive my parents, once and for all.

Before we parted ways in downtown Eugene, we snapped a photo, and then hugged and said goodbye. I didn't know when I might see him again.

Chapter 38

Year Seven:
August 2012

At 2 AM, on a Monday morning in August, David's cell phone rang on the nightstand. Exhausted from the visit to my parents' house, I rolled over and tried to go back to sleep. It was probably a call for David from someone at work.

The man on the phone sounded frantic. David suddenly sat upright in bed.

"What did they tell you about him?" I heard him ask. "Do you know what hospital he went to?"

My ears perked up. Could this have something to do with my father, who was one fall away from serious injury or death?. David pushed my shoulders. "Aaron, are you listening?"

David turned on the speakerphone. Right away, I realized the man on the phone had a Spanish accent. It was Rico's best friend, Cisco.

"No, the girl who called," Cisco replied, "She said she didn't know where they took him. I have been calling hospitals and the police. We can't figure out where he went."

"Was he drunk?" David asked. "Was he in an accident? Was he injured?"

No one could find Rico?

My worst nightmare, with Rico, had always been that he would make self-destructive choices that would wreck his chance at getting into the Navy, or that he might drive drunk and end up dead. My brother and I had high school friends who were killed as a result of driving straight off county roads after drinking. Their devastated parents went through absolute hell.

I tried to calm myself down. *Rico and I had talked about this. Rico had written about Freedom! He seemed to be coming around.* Was he making self-destructive choices on purpose? I pictured him in a cell somewhere, doing time, or working some a dead-end job.

David and I raced to our computers to look up phone numbers. We found the telephone number for the small-town Mollala police department. When we called, there was no answer.

David started dialing hospitals.

"This is David Douglas, I'm calling on behalf of a family who we think might have an injured family member there. They don't speak English well so I am trying to help them find their son, Rico. We think he may have been brought there. Could you check for me?"

He paused for a response.

"Last name Sanchez, first name Rico," said David.

"You do? Yes, thank you." He handed the phone to me. "You need to talk to them."

"Hello, I am the Big Brother of Rico Sanchez in the Big Brother/ Big Sister program. His mother doesn't speak English well and I am trying to help her find him. His friends think he may have been in an accident, but we don't know the extent of his injuries."

"Hold on please, sir," she said. There was a long pause.

"Hello," said a different woman's voice. "I'm the nurse taking care of Rico on the ward. He's here and he's OK. He is sleeping, and as soon as he is able to get up and walk out of here on his own, he is free to go."

"He's ok?"

"Yes," she said. "He's fine. He's sleeping. We are giving him fluids. He might be sleeping for several hours."

The nurse wouldn't give any more information. I thanked her, and then called Rico's mother with the name and address of the hospital. I rolled over and pulled the covers over my head.

"Aren't you going?" asked David.

"Fuck that! I have to work tomorrow. I'm going back to sleep." For hours I lay wide-awake and stared out the window at the high rises of Portland, worrying about Rico.

Early the next morning I called Rico's cell phone. It went straight to voicemail. With no idea what had happened, I left messages on his mother's phone. Because she was at work, she didn't answer. Several hours later, Rico finally called me back.

"What the hell?"

"Don't!" he wailed. "My head hurts."

"I thought you were dead! What is going on? Where were you?"

"At a party. I drank too much and blacked out."

He was just 18. With days left until he reported for the Navy, he couldn't afford a Minor in Possession charge.

"Were you driving? Did you get a ticket? The Navy won't take you if you got a ticket!"

He was insistent. "No! I didn't get a ticket!"

"Why didn't you answer your phone?"

"I lost it."

"How did you get to the hospital?"

"I don't know."

"Did your friends get tickets?"

"Yes."

"What were they for?" I demanded.

"I don't know," he said.

"Which of your friends were there? I want to call them to see what they remember."

"I've been calling them," he said. "They are all still sleeping."

"Cisco said you used a fake name."

There was silence.

"This is so messed up!" Before slamming down the phone I yelled, "I hope you enjoy your new career at Taco Bell!"

It concerned me that Rico might have been issued a citation. For the next 36 hours, I did Internet searches of court records. I also called my brother's wife, who was a court clerk in Eugene. She told me it was common for underage recruits to be caught drinking, but that they weren't always given tickets. She said they often called the court to see if a ticket was filed.

I called the Clackamas County Court and pretended to be Rico. No doubt I was the whitest-sounding 18-year-old Latino they'd ever spoken with.

"What's your date of birth?" she asked. I gave her Rico's birthday. Next she asked, "What's the incident date?"

"Last night," I said, "I was at a party with my friends. A lot of them got tickets, but I blacked out and went to the hospital, and I can't remember if I got one or not."

"What are some of your friends' names?" she asked.

I was stumped. I had no idea. I paused before replying. "I don't feel comfortable giving you any of their names."

I held my breath.

"Hold a minute," she said. I watched seconds tick by on the clock.

Finally, she came back. "I called the police department. They don't show any tickets for you. But they have a week to file them. Where can I reach you?"

I hung up on her.

If life had taught me anything, it was that it was impossible to control what was going to happen next.

As we waited to find out if Rico would be cited, things were tense between us. A week passed without a ticket. After a few weeks of not speaking to him, Rico called.

"I have to report for boot camp next week. Could you drop me off at the recruiter's? My mom can't take me."

"Why not?"

"Her car was stolen," he said.

"Stolen? Are you serious? When did this happen?"

"Last night."

"Did they break in?"

"No," he replied calmly, "she doesn't lock it."

"Oh," I said sarcastically, "maybe that's why they stole it!"

It felt, to me, more and more, that dropping Rico off at the recruiters would be my reward for years of hard work.

When I stopped by his apartment a few days later to pick him up, he told me he had been going through some of his things. He was trying to figure out what to dispose of before he left.

As we went through his closet, I discovered he had a story for every piece of clothing he owned. Rico had a memory associated with the place and time he bought things. He remembered who he was with, and could even recall how many times—and the places—he had worn something.

I stood next to him while he examined the few clothes he had accumulated in his young life. He reached in and pulled a blue hoodie off its hanger.

"Do you remember this?" he asked.

"It looks familiar…" Honestly though, one hoodie looked almost like another to me.

"This was the first thing you ever bought me," he said.

"Really? Okay," I agreed. Clearly he expected me to say more.

"Do you remember where we got it?"

"Top to Bottom?" I asked.

"No."

He seemed upset that I had forgotten. With pressure mounting, I started guessing. We had been to an awful lot of stores.

"Macy's?" I guessed.

"No, dumbass!"

"I give up," I said.

"We got it at Nordstrom Rack!" He was incredulous at my inability to recall the exact location. "Do you remember what you asked me when I asked you to buy this for me?"

"No…"

"You asked me if I really needed it."

I waited for him to add "…*asshole!*" He didn't, but it was obviously what he was thinking. *Of course he needed it,* but at the time I bought it, it meant Rico would have a new hoodie and the other two boys at his foster home would not. As nice as the idea was, I couldn't buy all of them clothes.

"I can't get rid of it," he said. "It means a lot to me." I stared at the hoodie. It was a funny thing: I had been forced into a closet my whole life, but this was the first time I felt beloved in one.

A few days later, I arrived at his house to chauffeur him three miles to the recruiter's office.

"I have to stop by the court on the way," he said. "I have to get proof that those old tickets are gone so the Navy will accept me." With hours to spare, Rico had completed the traffic safety course required to erase his citations. Now all that was left was to get the violations dismissed in the next 40 minutes.

The courthouse was on the way to the Navy recruiter's office, and there was no one waiting in line. Given that an entire season of the TV shows *Cops* was filmed in Rico's neighborhood of Rockwood, it surprised me to see the place nearly empty. His citations were duly dismissed, and off we sped to the recruiter's.

It seemed that paperwork was never done. Paperwork had brought us together and now it was paperwork that would separate us.

I pulled into the Navy's parking lot. Rico hopped out of the car.

"I'll call you later," he said.

So that was it? I don't know what else I expected, really. I guess I thought he might have gotten out, put his arm across the top of the car peered down at the wise Big Brother he had come to trust and respect and said:

"Hey, I would really like to thank you. Thank you for all of the Saturdays sitting on hard, uncomfortable bleachers for hours only to see me wrestle for a total of eight minutes, with only an occasional nod—and sometimes a glare—from me. Thank you for understanding that when I was being an ass I was just being a normal teenager. Thank you for knowing that we all go through stages in life that really suck, and for knowing this was my time. Thank you for encouraging me to do better in school and telling me that I could make something of myself. And thank you for telling me you loved me (no homo) because even though you are as queer as any fag ever gets, you are my big fag brother and that makes you special to me."

I heaved a sigh as Rico walked through the recruiter's front door.

As my car backed out, Rico re-emerged with a tall man in a tan uniform. He led him around the corner of the building. Their conversation looked very serious. The uniformed man waved papers around as he flipped through them.

I held my breath. Was Rico being rejected? They rounded the corner, until nothing was visible but the recruiter's gesticulating hands. Were these kind hands? Mean hands? What were they saying?

I slowly pulled the Saab into the middle of the parking lot and turned off the engine, hoping to hide unseen. Three minutes later, the recruiter led Rico back into the office. In a few minutes, when he didn't come out again, I started breathing normally.

A few hours later my phone rang.

"Hello?"

"What are you doing?" asked Rico.

"Watching the news. What are *you* doing? I thought you were on your way to Chicago?"

"Oh, no—I'm playing basketball with Cisco and a bunch of my friends..."

"WHAT? What are you doing there? Aren't you supposed to be at home base or whatever they call it?"

"Nooooo! I got a pass until 10:00," he said. "I was wondering if you could come pick me up about 9:30?"

Oh dear God! I'm not done yet?

As I drove to pick him up for what I hoped to be the last time before boot camp, I wondered if he'd finally have anything real to talk about. Perhaps there was something he hadn't had the courage to say; maybe he might say in the last 30 seconds of our last half hour.

It was dark when I picked him up. We stopped at Target to get some frozen yogurt and a couple of Red Bulls. He didn't say much.

"My mom cried when she dropped me off to play basketball this evening."

"Really? Aww. That's sad," I said.

"Yeah, and my sister told me she was going to miss me," he said. "She cried too."

"Very sweet," I said almost coldly. "Of course they're going to miss you." *I just want you to know your ass is on that plane!*

We cruised across the open blacktop of the Holiday Inn parking lot and approached our final destination. Its entrance was under construction, the doors hidden by scaffolding, ladders, and debris.

Rico turned to me. "I don't want my little brother to have to join the military," he said. "I don't think that would be right for him."

"I know. We started a college savings plan for him already."

Rico frowned. "How come you didn't do that for me?"

The young man whom I had spent so much time with, over the past six years, was about to step through a door, and out of my life, as a grown man. The next morning, he and the other recruits would board a plane to the Recruit Training Command at Great Lakes, Illinois. Who knew what kind of transformation was in store—what might emerge after nine weeks of boot camp?

He opened the car door and stepped out.

"Thanks for the ride. I'll call you. I'll write." He turned and sat back down in the car. He flung an arm around me and said: "I'm going to miss you, faggot."

He said these words because he accepted and loved me. Words that had been painful slurs in junior high had become forever powerless over me.

What stung now was my realization that Rico didn't need me anymore. Just as I had packed my bags and left home so many years earlier, Rico was off on his own adventures. My adventures in the 1980s had been without boundaries. Rico would still have some kind of adventures, thought they would be controlled by Uncle Sam. Given his history, it seemed like a good option for the next few years.

Chapter 39

Letting Go

A few months later I ran across the Training Manual from Big Brothers/Big Sisters. I flipped through it, trying to find the answer to a new question that had been really bothering me. As I scanned the index, something important seemed missing.

There was no lesson on letting go.

Friends move, family passes. Little Brothers grow up. They have lives and careers of their own, and they stop depending on you for help. You don't see them every week any longer.

During my friendship with Rico, we had all kinds of paperwork. First was our Friendship Agreement. During the intervening years, we'd had liability releases for him and his friends. I'd filled out paperwork for travel, school enrollment, athletics, the state and medical paperwork. I'd written a hundred reports and emails on his progress, and completed surveys on our match experience. There was a paper trail for pretty much everything.

Paperwork is risk-avoidant. It releases someone from liability. But it says nothing about emotions. It says nothing about worries, fears, hopes, aspirations, or caring. The emotional part of our relationship could not be certified on a document. Our relationship, codified by paper, lacked any legal protections of parenthood.

Parenthood was a privilege I could never have. Parents got the presumption of privilege, regardless whether they were good at it, or never showed up at all.

I had no rights. I had to earn Rico's respect. Our relationship always seemed tenuous.

At 17, I desperately wanted to file the necessary paperwork to get rid of my parents. Rico wanted the opposite.

Rico and I had gone from *You're amazing!* to *You make my life awful!* Now that he was leaving, I surprised myself with feelings of *wait—don't go!*

After taking care of a ton of paperwork for Rico, he was out of my life.

I didn't realize how much I would miss him.

There was solace in knowing I wasn't the only one missing Rico. His younger brother Luis longed for him too. When Rico left, Luis was just 10 years old. On his Facebook wall he wrote, "Talking to the moon. Can't believe my brother is gone."

At boot camp, they shaved Rico's head, gave him a uniform and made him pack all his old clothes and belongings into a box. They mailed it home to his mother.

That's how you knew the military owned you.

I sent Rico a letter:

September 15, 2012

Dear brother:

I hope that everything is going well with you. I can't believe it's already been a couple of weeks now since you left. From what I read about boot camp from Google was that weeks 3-8 were a lot more interesting than the first two. And it seemed like the last two were the most intense. I am looking forward to hearing more about your daily routine.

David is so nice to Luis all the time. It's REALLY easy for me to say no to him but it was not always so easy with you. I tried to always say no a few times before I said yes, which is when you probably figured out at one point that if you just asked enough times for that extra 20 bucks I would change my mind! I had to be sure you really needed it.

This is the holiest part of the entire year for Jews, who basically attend a confession together. It is a time for reflection and to ask everyone we know for forgiveness. And so, as I may have done in years past, it is time now for me to say that *if I have said or done anything that offended you in the past year, I regret it.* And I really mean that. I would appreciate your forgiveness if I have, because I hope you know that has never been my intention and I have only the highest regard and the highest hopes for you and your future.

Well, I should sign off now. Hope you have a good next few weeks. We're all thinking about you and are looking forward to having you back to visit.

Love from your brother,

–Aaron

He wrote me back, and said he was thinking about my parents. He was realizing how fast time goes by, and that parents aren't around forever. He said he'd had time to think about his relationship with his mother. He was sorry they fought so much. He said he had written his mother, telling her he hoped she was proud of him, and that he hoped his being in the Navy was setting a good example for his brothers.

I wrote Rico almost every week of boot camp. Before we knew it, he had his graduation. His mother, sister, foster parents and I flew to Chicago to attend the ceremony.

After the ceremony, I led his family through the crowd. His sister got her first glimpse of him and started to cry. Rico smiled at her. He flung his arms around his foster dad's neck and cried tears of joy. I knew James' influence had led to Rico's decision to join the Navy; Rico wanted James to be proud of him. It was rare to see his emotional side. After a minute, James gently pushed Rico away. Then Rico hugged his mother and sister, and shook my hand.

On the way to lunch, Rico recounted details about the designations of rank on emblems and patches. I remarked at how much he seemed to have learned in boot camp. He turned to me and matter-of-factly stated:

"I feel like I've been brainwashed."

He went on to explain that he hated his uniform pants because there were so many buttons—they were hard to loosen with a full bladder. The trousers were a far cry from the low-hanging jeans he used to wear.

After lunch we went back to the hotel. Rico went to his mother's room to take a nap. I rested my forehead against the closed door of my room and heaved a sigh. There was something I still needed to talk to him about.

I had recently interviewed for a new Little Brother. Rico didn't know I had already gone through orientation. It felt as if I were cheating on him. Was it right to talk to him about it? Losing him to the world was like losing a part of myself.

Wasn't this what I had always wanted?

I sat down on the bed, put my head in my hands, and cried. I felt so much a part of this family. It was impossible to imagine having the same feeling with another Little Brother. With all the language and cultural barriers, it had taken years to integrate, and we still had a way to go. Did I really want to start all over?

Nothing prepared me for the striking feelings of loneliness after Rico moved away. It was different than what I'd experienced when good friends left. *Who would I lecture? Who would take pleasure in ignoring my advice? Who would call me a fag?*

Our friendship wasn't caused by any natural course of life events. Without Big Brothers/Big Sisters, we would never have met. Maybe that's why my relationship with Rico meant so much to me. We forged bonds, despite our inherent differences in a society that normally would have kept us apart.

Another reason made me sad, although it took time to completely understand it. For all the time I had spent with Rico—for all my time encouraging, lecturing, and trying to understand him—I really didn't know him all that well. The same cloud of unknowing that existed between any parent and child was the same barrier that might always stand between Rico and me. Despite a lifetime of interactions with my own parents, I didn't feel they really knew that much about my life. I knew Rico as well as I ever could. Maybe consistency would give me one advantage over the average parent—Rico could never say I wasn't there for him.

The day after Rico graduated from boot camp, he called.

"Thank you for being there."

"I wouldn't have missed it."

"Yes, you would have."

Where was that coming from?

"No," I repeated in my most serious tone of voice, "I wouldn't have."

Next, he gave me a long list of items he wanted me to ship to him aboard his aircraft carrier, the *U.S.S. Harry S. Truman.*

I heard noise in the background. "Wait!" he said. It sounded like someone was talking over a loudspeaker. There was a lot of chatter. He came back on the phone.

"What was that?" I asked.

"There was an announcement," he said. "When there is an announcement, I have to listen."

Apparently, a person of authority had a control room where they called on various recruits to do various jobs. These announcements came about every 60 seconds. This had the purpose of forcing the new recruits to pay attention and stay alert. It happened with such frequency that I began to ignore it. He finally said matter-of-factly, "It doesn't matter if you keep talking when I say 'wait a minute.' I stop hearing anything that you're saying."

Not that he ever listened to me before! But Rico seemed more serious now. I realized I didn't have to be his father or Big Brother anymore. The military would take care of that.

A week later, we talked on the phone in his mom's apartment, as I packed up clothes to send him.

He asked, "Have I told you lately that I love you, brother?"

"No," I replied, tearing up a little, "but you can tell me now."

"You're the best Big Brother anyone could ever have."

~   ~   ~

After a few months, things got easier. I began to feel more myself again—and not like a piece of me had been taken away.

Another part of my life was in transition, as well. While I had grieved the loss of Rico's presence, my father's health had taken a sudden turn for the worse.

Chapter 40

Saying Goodbye: January 2013

Since the fall, when Rico left for boot camp, my trips home to Springfield increased to almost every weekend. My visits were about the only time Dad got a shower. He was disinclined to take them, and no one else wanted to manage him in the tub.

His care had grown more complicated. We had to make sure he was using his oxygen, and he needed special drops put in his eyes frequently so they wouldn't dry out. Though it was a little awkward, there was something comforting in taking care of him. It felt like we had reached some resolution for all the years of hurt and anger.

Dad had recently gone to the hospital after he fell and hit his head again on the white brick fireplace. He had a few weeks of rehab afterward in a care center to make sure he was OK to go home. Several times a day he insisted on returning to his own living room as soon as possible, and my mother said she wanted to keep caring for him.

Dad was officially put on hospice care, which meant no extraordinary measures would be taken to prolong his life, and that he could be given medications to ease any pain he might have. The designation meant Medicare would cover the cost of a hospital bed at his home as well as some nursing visits.

I visited a day or two after Dad was back at home. He was in a hospital bed, set up in my parents' bedroom. I was shocked to see how pale and gaunt he had become.

As I entered the room, he sensed my presence.

"Hello... Aaron?" he asked.

"Hi Dad," I replied.

"You're a long way from home! How're you doin', sonny? Gosh it's good to see you."

It was then I realized: *this is my dad, and I'm watching him die.*

I thought about that sand hole at the beach, when I was six years old—when it seemed that he just stood there as I was being sucked through the Earth all the way to China.

Now I was the one watching. He had fallen, and I stood by as he was being sucked into the void. There was nothing I could do to save him.

I sat on the hospital bed, leaned over, and wept with my head on his chest.

"I love you, Dad," I sobbed.

He touched my head. "You were always a good boy. I love you too, son."

Rico didn't have a dad, but I did. Rico didn't know it, but he had helped me learn how to be a better son. At least my dad had loved me, in his own way. It had taken me all these years to see that.

"I want you to promise me something," he said.

"What?" I asked, barely lifting my head.

"I want you to take care of your mother for me."

"Okay, Dad. Okay."

"I want you to promise me."

"I will, Dad. I promise."

~   ~   ~

Mom waited in the living room. She desperately needed to sleep. For the next four nights, she slept in her room while I stayed in the living room, with dad camped out next to me in his forest green La-Z-Boy.

Those were some of the hardest nights of my life. How could my frail mother have taken care of Dad, all by herself, for so many months?

Dad's blindness caused him to confuse day for night. He slept all day and was up, off and on, into the wee hours. About every 90 minutes he needed help to the toilet. Each time he got up out of his chair to use the walker, we slowly rolled down their long hallway, while I tried to keep his oxygen tube from getting tangled up in the wheels or on the handles. Dad didn't always make it to the toilet in time.

By the third night, I had become angry at him for waking me up so much. Lack of sleep had me disoriented. I had to remind myself about all the years he had taken care of me. Now, life had given me the opportunity to return the favor.

After a few days, I had to go back to work. On the day before I left, Alan, Denise and I got together with Mom. We decided that there was no way she could take care of Dad by herself. He needed to go back into the nursing home—at least until we knew more about his current medical needs.

Mom needed more rest. I was afraid this intensive caregiving might literally kill her. We found what we believed was the best possible nursing home in Eugene, and got Dad a private room there.

We all knew Dad would die soon. We were told his body was starting to shut down. David and I spent a lot of time visiting Dad in the nursing home. The weather was consistently dark and moody.

I distracted myself by working on a slide show, a memorial service flyer and his obituary. It seemed morbid, but I was a journalism graduate. One of the basics of journalism was to learn the importance of preparing obituaries far in advance. Pre-written obits could be stowed away for years, then quickly finalized when needed. It could be difficult to get an accurate, meaningful and factual obituary written at the last minute. I also wanted my siblings' approval on what should appear in the paper. It was unimaginable to think of working on this while I was grieving.

After Dad had been in the nursing home for a few weeks, his condition became more serious. Unusual things began to happen. One day, he reached his arms up from the bed at a 90-degree angle, dragging up the sheets and covers with them, like a bedridden Frankenstein. About a half hour later the hospice nurse—a former Army caregiver who had assisted the dying for over 20 years—came in.

"Pretty soon he's going to start doing the arm ballet," she said. "They reach out and try to touch things that we can't see, but they can."

"He just did that!" I said.

"Yeah," she replied, "that's pretty typical about three or four days before they pass over." Then she said, "He'll start seeing or talking to dead people that he knows."

A few days later, Dad woke up out of what seemed like a deep sleep. "I just saw Jerry Lake drive by in the parking lot," he cried. "He's been dead for years!"

Dad was completely blind. He hadn't seen the parking lot.

My brother, sister and I sat with Mom in Dad's room for an entire week. We left only to go home for dinner and to sleep.

One evening, as we all sat there, Dad suddenly awoke from his slumber and sat straight up in bed.

"Who's here?" he demanded.

"Aaron," I said.

"Denise," said my sister.

"Alan," said my brother.

Mom squeezed his hand. "Emily," she said.

"What are you all doing here?" he asked loudly, "*sitting around waiting for me to die?*"

We looked at each other in stunned silence. Dad was absolutely right. That was the day we decided to stop waiting. I went back to work. Dad lived for several more weeks.

During the days and nights of caring for my father, I took some time to write to Rico.

Dear Rico,

I don't know whether I have ever really expressed to you how incredibly proud I am of what you have made of yourself and how much you mean to me. You know, when you have a parent living in a nursing home, with days numbered, things really change. You spend hours thinking about all your interactions with them, hoping that you said everything you really needed to or ever wanted. What's weird is that we wait often times to do this until they are in their waning years or moments. Perhaps they are something less than their original selves, and their souls will never completely understand the things that you say to them. You can regret the fact that you waited so long to tell people close to you the things you were feeling.

When I was growing up—my dad never told me he loved me. Not one time as far as I remember. No one in our family was ever particularly affectionate, which in some ways I don't think is such a great idea. I've learned that it is important to talk about your feelings with people. Even if by talking you just sit down and write a two-page letter to someone in the military.

I mean, you have to let people know what you really think, because this is life right now today, it's not a dress rehearsal for another time later. We never know which day is going to be the last, so we should always live today as if this were the last day we will ever have.

I was thinking today about your girlfriend; I was really glad you had that experience. Whatever the situation might have been it was nice to see you so happy and being silly and just having a fun time. It would be nice to see you be like that again some day.

That said, I don't think there's a huge necessity for you to be settling down anytime soon. Just be careful and don't do anything stupid and everything will be ok. And by careful I mean prostitutes have STDs. There are plenty of college girls giving it away, there's no need to pay for it!

And some day when you do find that perfect girl you will just know it, and you'll make a great husband and father.

I was a little surprised when you asked me the other day whether you were really that big a part of my life. And I thought "really you're asking me that question?" But maybe I never really did say not that just I love you Rico, but that you are one of the most important things in my life.

With love from your brother.

–Aaron

לברכה זיכרונו[1]

On March 5, 2013, Dad died while Mom sat holding his hand.

There was a graveside service two days later. It had been raining for days, but the weather cleared in time for the service. The immediate family and our spouses rode with Mom in Alan's SUV. We carried Dad's coffin and laid it to rest. I was the only one of the immediate family who spoke. I read a lovely, mournful, Jewish prayer.

After the service, as we rode away, I sat in the back seat next to Mom. She held my hand as the sun streamed into the car. When we got back to the house, I went straight to the bedroom I had shared with my brother. Although Springfield is often foggy and dank in March, that day the sun shone straight through the window onto the bedspread. I lay down and cried, trying to absorb the fact that Dad was really gone. Now Mom would be alone.

After all the days of darkness and rain while he had been in the nursing home, this day, though sad, was filled with warmth and sun and the promise of spring.

I talked aloud to Dad then. "I'm going to miss you, Dad." I looked out the window. As if for the first time, I noticed a trio of white birdhouses Dad had built for Mom. They were on a pedestal about nine feet high, framed artistically by the window. Above the birdhouses was a sign he had painted: "This place is for the birds."

"Yes... yes it is," I thought.

---

1   Hebrew: May his memory be a blessing.

By the time we held his public memorial, a week later, I had prepared some remarks. A large crowd of former co-workers, family members, and students filled the auditorium at Thurston High. The people who wanted to talk about my dad included a fellow teacher, a coach, and one of the kids from the cul-de-sac, who broke down in tears talking about the things Dad had taught him. I spoke in general terms:

> My dad was a man who knew how to fish, hunt, flirt
> and lecture. He believed that it was just a matter
> of the right lecture at the right time that could set a
> wayward youth onto the path of self-sustenance.
>
> Over the years he worked on his theory, mainly with
> his own children, but frequently with the thousands
> of students at school—often with some success.
> Whenever his theory or lecture failed to work,
> though, he could ruminate over it for weeks, years, or
> even decades. And rarely did my father ruminate in
> silence.
>
> I'm going to miss him, and I'll even miss his lectures.

A couple of weeks after the memorial service, I shared the news of Dad's death with Rico. It was a difficult letter to write.

March 19, 2013

Dear Rico:

On March 5th, Dad died. I haven't really had much of a chance to grieve. For weeks and months before, I had to work on collecting insurance for the nursing home, help Mom around the house, and even visit the funeral home, write an obituary, and prepare a program for his memorial service. There wasn't much time to think about him leaving us forever.

I feel numb now somehow but I know that eventually that will wear off...sort of. When your friends and family die, you somehow lose a part of yourself that you know you won't have back in exactly the same way.

The part of the service that really got to me was when the Oregon National Guard Honor Guard came and unfolded and folded the flag and a trumpeter played taps. They handed my mom the flag and said "On behalf of the President of the United States, I present you with this American flag in honor of your husband's service to his country."

Love, your brother,

–Aaron

PS I am glad to hear you have a mentor on the ship. It's good to have lots of mentors throughout life. Everyone will teach you something different.

PS2 I've changed my will and you are in it now.

PS3 I plan to live a really, really long time.

Rico sent me a note thanking me for the memorial service program, although it left him deeply saddened.

After that, Rico and I spoke often by phone, and texted several times a week. One time I asked whether he remembered what we did on our first outing.

"We drove to a park and played Frisbee together," he said. "It was a Frisbee of mine that said U.S. Navy on it. That's kind of ironic, don't you think?"

Life had been full of little ironies. The biggest of all had been the change I'd seen in my own mother.

Chapter 41

Emily

As the years passed, my mother's reaction to the idea of my being gay completely changed. Indeed, I think she grew to enjoy it. At the same time, her taste in TV became almost raunchy. Long gone were *Days of our Lives* and *General Hospital*. They had been replaced with endless reruns of *CSI*. Her favorite TV shows now featured overtly gay characters: *Project Runway, The Voice, Queer Eye for the Straight Guy*, chef cook-offs and numerous restaurant and home makeover shows.

Mom watches them all from the comfort of her red padded O-ring on the end of the couch nearest the kitchen, where it's easy for her to catch the phone or run to the restroom. Her Chihuahua, Patches, sits next to her, parked beneath the same gold spray-painted cherubs that hung on the wall 25 years ago, on the night I declared "I'm gay." On my monthly weekend visits, we have ample time to watch many of her favorites.

In the summer of 2014, a show called *Epic Ink* premiered on A&E. It featured a Springfield tattoo shop called Area 51. Although she was 82 years old at the time, Mom stayed up past her 10:30 PM bedtime to catch the show's world premiere.

After the first 15 minutes, she was beside herself with glee. "This is really putting Springfield on the map!" she beamed.

I grimaced as I watched the show's grungy arm-sleeved multi-pierced artists speak in short phrases peppered with bleeped f-bombs. "That's for sure!"

As a teenager, it would have been inconceivable that my conservative Republican mother might one day exclaim her love for a TV show about a cadre of cursing Springfield tattoo artists—much less proclaim civic pride over it.

One night she asked me to watch her favorite show "How to Get Away with Murder." It turned out to be a drama so graphic in its weekly gay sex scenes that it was basically soft-core porn.

Mom doesn't miss an episode. It's hard to decide whether it's because she likes the storyline or the gratuitous gay sex.

Chapter 42

Year Nine: January 2015

Rico's plane was scheduled to land at Portland International Airport around midnight one Saturday evening. He asked me if I would pick him up.

"Gee, that's pretty late," I said. "You're going home, right? Wouldn't you like to have your Mom pick you up?"

"No," he said. "Come get me, please?"

Rico was chatty that night. He had just turned 21. One of his flights had been delayed and he spent a couple of hours drinking in an airport bar.

When Rico arrived home his mother was in the kitchen. She hugged him, laughing and saying "Pendejo!" (*stupid*). I sighed, and felt a little sorry for him. His worst memory, growing up, had been when he crashed his bike into a telephone pole. His mother called him stupid then. Today he visited her from the Navy, and it was the first word out of her mouth. Maybe it was her term of endearment for him, much like his use of "faggot" for me.

A few days earlier, when a friend of mine heard Rico was coming home for a visit, he offered me his tickets to a Portland Trailblazers game. Rico and I hadn't been to a game together in years.

What Rico didn't know is that I had nominated him to be the Hometown Hero—the local military member who is honored on national TV, while 19,000 Trailblazer fans at the packed Moda Center watch from inside the arena. A few glitches nearly derailed my plan to keep it a surprise—including signs taped to our seats that said: "Welcome Hometown Hero! Please remain seated during the third quarter."

From behind me, Rico watched as I pulled the signs off the chairs and tossed them on the floor.

"What did those signs say?" he asked.

"Oh, just my friend Joe leaving us a note saying he hopes we have a good time using his tickets" I was glad Rico stopped asking questions.

During the third quarter, a man wearing a headset motioned to me from the aisle. I got up to talk to him. He moved up the stairs a bit, and I followed.

"Does he still not know what's going on?" asked the man.

"He has absolutely no idea," I said.

"OK. We'll put the camera on him when we're ready to go. Don't go anywhere."

I returned to my seat. Rico asked, "What did he want?"

"Oh, I forgot to tell you that I entered you into the contest to win a new car if you make a shot from half court," I said. "He said they are going to pull one of you down to do that in a few minutes."

"But I really have to pee."

"Well, you can't go anywhere right now! You have to stay right here! If you're not in your seat they won't let you make the shot."

"Ugg," he said. "It's killing me!"

I wore a zippered sweatshirt to the game, so I could quickly reveal my Big Brothers/Big Sisters T-Shirt that said "It's BIG time!"

As part of the preparation, I had e-mailed photos of Rico in uniform with his family, along with this paragraph for the announcer:

> U.S. Navy seaman Rico Sanchez is surprised to
> learn that he's tonight's Hometown Hero! Home
> for the holidays and to celebrate his 21st birthday
> with family, Rico works as an Aviation Support
> Equipment Technician aboard one of the world's
> largest aircraft carriers. . .

As his name was read, and the first picture showed up on the Jumbo Tron, bright lights shined in his face.

Rico turned to me and asked, "What's happening right now?"

"Wave to the camera!" I replied, "You're the Hometown Hero!"

Rico smiled and waved as the announcer continued:

> …When he completes his tour of duty in two
> years, he plans to major in computer science at the
> University of Oregon and work in the healthcare
> industry. Rico is here tonight with his Big Brother
> who tells us he is incredibly proud of the man Rico
> has become over the past nine years.

The crowd roared with applause. After we sat down, Rico leaned over and gave me a hug.

"Thank you," he said, "I appreciate it."

This time, I hugged him back.

Photo Courtesy: Greg Frick

Chapter 43

Rewind: Two Years Earlier

In the days before Rico's high school graduation, I mentioned my interest in getting another Little Brother.

"I think I have one more in me," I said.

He said nothing about it until the following week, when he looked at me seriously and said:

"I know you said you want to get another brother, but I don't want to be replaced."

"You know there's no one who can replace you. But there are so many boys out there who are like you were when you were twelve years old. Think of them."

"David is Luis's Big Brother. Can't you help him out?"

"It's not the same."

"What about Diego?" he asked. "He needs a Big Brother."

"He's only four years old."

Several months later, after our trip to Chicago for Rico's boot camp graduation, Maria caught a ride home with me from the airport.

At about 9 PM, we stopped to pick up Diego at the babysitter's. Maria emerged from the sitter's apartment with his car seat in one hand. In the other arm she held Diego, who was sound asleep, over her shoulder.

After we arrived outside Maria's apartment, she went to a neighbor to wake up Luis.

I stepped out of the car. It was raining gently as I opened the door to the back seat. I looked down at Diego, asleep in the back seat.

"You probably can't hear me," I said, "and you don't know it yet, but we're going to have some adventures, you and me."

Maria and Luis were approaching, from across the parking lot, as I spoke. I had things I wanted to say to my new Little Brother.

"I mean, you're pretty stubborn, even now. But I think you'll grow up to do great things."

I reached into the back seat and lifted Diego over my shoulder. I carried him across the parking lot, upstairs to his room. After tucking him in bed, I turned to go.

So much had happened over the past few years. I didn't feel like a brother, or like a parent. Parents don't get to start over. I could never replace Rico; I knew this time would be different.

This time, I wouldn't try to be a parent. This time, I wouldn't worry about being a Brother. This time I would be a friend—and a member of the family—from the very beginning.

I took one last look at the sleeping boy. As I turned to go, I switched off the light.

THE END

Postscript

- In 2014, Rico's sister Gabriela became a U.S. citizen.

- In 2015, David's Little Brother Luis made honor roll, broke a school track record and won the district championship in the 1,500 meters.

- Russell lives east of Springfield, where he works as a general contractor and plays piano at the local church.

- In June, 2015, same-sex marriage became legal in all 50 states.

- After three years of legal paperwork, Rico's mother obtained her work permit and will soon have a green card.

- After his tour of duty is up, Rico plans to return to Portland to attend college.

There is power in unconditional love.
Its transformative nature has made all the difference
for Rico and me.

Let it in!

Acknowledgements

Thanks to editors Frank M. Young and Arthur Manzi and all my project readers and those who offered encouragement and assistance- including but not limited to: Anna Arredondo, Barbara York Baker, Jennifer Brandlon, Jenn Director-Knudsen, Dallen Esselstrom, Greg Frick, Brenda Higley, Liza McQuade, Jennifer Johnson, Vanessa Nix Anthony, with special thanks to Jordan Crawford for his insight, encouragement, and assistance. Thanks also to the team at HFO Investment Real Estate. Much love to my husband David M. Douglas for his encouragement, kindness, and for traveling alongside me.

Photo Courtesy: AshleyPrieur

About the Author – Aaron Kirk Douglas

Aaron Kirk Douglas is a Journalism graduate of the University of Oregon and has been marketing director at some of the largest and most prominent law firms in the Pacific Northwest.

For the past eight years in addition to working full time marketing commercial real estate, Mr. Douglas has completed several documentary film projects including the award-winning *Monster Camp*. He has a new musical project in development with Broadway conductor Kurt Crowley which has been supported by several production companies and artistic grants.

Mr. Douglas is a board member of Big Brothers/Big Sisters Columbia Northwest. In 2015, he was a top three finalist for national mentoring competition from The National Mentoring Partnership. In 2011, he received one of Oregon's highest individual honors for outstanding personal achievement in volunteerism in support of low-income children and families, and in 2010 he was a nominee for National Big Brother of The Year.

He lives in Portland with his husband David and their pets ZigZag and Ranger.

C 70